11.3.60

Augustus "Gus" Belt, (l) Steak n Shakes's founder, views a cake made for the opening of a St. Louis store (9009 Riverview Blvd.) in 1953. Steak n Shake president John Engle accompanies Mr. Belt.

SELLING STEAKBURGERS

The Growth of a Corporate Culture

Robert P. Cronin

President, Steak n Shake, Inc. 1971-1981
Chairman 1971-1984

Guild Press of Indiana, Inc.
Carmel, Indiana

TABLE OF CONTENTS

Dedication vi

Overture vii

Chapter 1: "Get Your Kicks on Route 66" 1

Chapter 2: "Let's Have Another Cup of Coffee and Let's
        Have Another Piece of Pie" 7

Chapter 3: "Accentuate the Positive"—Gus Belt 22

Chapter 4: The Saint Louis Blue Skies 26

Chapter 5: "Can't Get Indiana Off My Mind" 33

Chapter 6:"It Don't Mean a Thing if It Ain't Got That
        Swing"—Quality, Cleanliness and Service 41

Chapter 7: Steady as She Grows 57

Chapter 8: The Customer Is Always Right 69

Chapter 9: Spreading the Gospel According to Gus 81

Chapter10: "Back Home Again in Indiana" 87

Chapter11: Show Me State Steak n Shakes 90

Chapter12: "You Are My Sunshine" 93

Chapter13: Seven Come Fifty (States That Is) 100

Chapter14: "Someone's Rocking My Dreamboat" 105

Chapter 15: "The Best Is Yet to Come . . ." 109

"Dedicated to You"

This book is dedicated to all the employees of Steak n Shake in the fifteen states it serves. You and thousands of others who have come before you have dedicated yourselves to giving customers the kind of unique food service Mr. Gus Belt conceived of back in 1934. You form a human chain, past and present, of caring in business, and you are both the strength and promise of the chain.

I especially want to recognize, commend and thank my good friend Herb Leonard, who has been associated with Steak n Shake for over sixty years, for being as big a booster as the company has ever had, and for being a great contributor and inspiration in helping me produce this book.

Overture

When I went in 1946 to law school at Indiana University in Bloomington, one of the new friends I made was Jens D. Moller. He operated a hamburger joint called "Next to the Best." When I asked J.D. why he called his restaurant "Next to the Best" he said, "Because Steak n Shake is the best." That was the first time I heard of Steak n Shake.

Interestingly enough, I had not been in a Steak n Shake when I was presented with the opportunity of buying control of the chain. Of course I had seen many of the restaurants; who could miss the sight of those clean, white places you caught out of the corner of your eyes as you drove through business and residential areas. What, I wondered, was that odd Indian word on pink neon signs in front of the things?

I was particularly aware for years of one Steak n Shake at 3810 W. Washington in Indianapolis which I passed as I went to the Weir Cook Municipal Airport. The store name seemed odd. Steak *and* Shake? How would a steak go with a shake? Steak n Martini would be better, I thought.

In May of 1971, a financial adviser and I went to lunch at the Steak n Shake on Keystone Avenue in Indianapolis. Broadly smiling pretty girls with short skirts and jaunty caps were hustling to the cars in the parking lot under a sign marked "Curb Service." But we were heading for a meal inside, so we stepped through the door.

A sign on the door said "No shoes, No shirt, No service." I think Steak n Shake originated that order. Once inside I immediately loved the clean, crisp black and white decor, suggestive of everyone's ideal of the eatery of their dreams. Appealing "steakburgers" quickly arrived, seared on the outside, buns toasted, with ample pickles and juicy onions. Shoestring fries were piled high enough to fall off the plate. This wasn't your normal "greasy spoon." The only touch that seemed a little off was the presence of little white packages of ketchup and mustard. But the waitress smiled down at me, with a wide smile, and put down the creamy chocolate shake, and I forgot everything else. Nice, well-run little eatery of my dreams.

It was the beginning of a long romance through many states which reached well beyond the many hundreds of Steak n Shake steakburgers I have sunk my teeth into since that time. I bought control of the company in 1971, not long after the founder's family had sold it. I ran it through years which saw phenomenal growth and the development of a corporate culture. That little string of drive-ins grew into a chain of restaurants which have held their own and grown steadily through the tidal wave of McDonald's and pizza places which has washed over America since then.

This is a story of how "the people's choice" among hamburger places grew into one of the significant restaurant presences in America—a corporate force and a cultural icon. Billions of steakburgers were not sold, as the signs at the rival place state, but millions have been well and carefully made to suit the public taste and *eaten*. This is the story of that effort— the "nothing but the best" of the hamburger world, served one steakburger at a time.

CHAPTER ONE

"GET YOUR KICKS ON ROUTE 66"
—Bobby Troup

Steak n Shake sprang out of the tradition of the American diner. It was born during the Depression, which made the call for fast, quick and inexpensive roadside restaurant food a necessity.

The 1930s saw the growth of diners alongside the roads of America, which, in spite of the economic scene, were experiencing brisk traffic, as the family automobile began to experience its heyday. Originally established in actual dining cars retired from a declining railroad industry, small restaurant diners served quickly prepared food for hungry travelers.

Father, mother, a couple of kids and perhaps an aunt piled into the Model-A on their way to visit Grandma, seeking cheap entertainment in a "Sunday afternoon auto ride." They could not afford to go into the fancy city or hotel restaurants alongside the two-lane highways which served as the paths from place to place. They could pack a lunch, but a stopoff at Joe's Cafe, or Myra's Coffee Cup with the big Coke bottle sign in front of it, provided a meal in an economical and often satisfying way.

The narrow width of the long dining car format quickly "took wings," expanding sideways, as increased traffic demanded more spacious dining. Several shapes evolved from teepees to coffeepots with metal spouts, but the diner even in its expanded form stayed small and cozy, specializing in short orders, sandwiches, french and American fries, and pie. For liquid refreshment there was beer, lots of coffee, and the Coca Colas, Dr. Peppers and other fizzing drinks Americans had come to love.

In 1921 White Castle became the first "chain" hamburger restaurant operation. It featured small hamburgers with onions and drinks and a clean, white decor to emphasize cleanliness in its operation. The Howard Johnson Coffee Shop chain also began in 1921.

Enter Gus Belt.

As I picked up the reins of Steak n Shake in 1971, I quickly came to understand just how important the founder of the chain had been. Oldtimers in the Steak n Steak corporation— many of whom had been with the chain since its founding days—treated their founder with a reverence that bordered on awe.

Augustus Hamilton Belt, better known as Gus, was truly an American small business icon and a master of the skill of marketing if there ever was one. If you believed half the stories that were still circulating around Steak n Shake fifteen or more years after his death, you could see you were dealing with somebody unusual—sort of halfway between Will Rogers and James Cash Penney.

Gus was a native of a small town near Springfield, Illinois. He had acquired the General Tire distributorship, servicing cars in Irvington, Indiana, traveling and selling tires and even managing a tire store at one point. The tire business did not prosper for him. During the Depression General Tire and the automobile industry in general, had several ups and downs, and Gus found himself bankrupt and out of a job. After trying, and failing, in a steakhouse operation and a couple of other things, he finally managed to acquire a Shell Oil station at 1219 S. Main in Normal, Illinois, just north of Bloomington on the famous Route 66.

People like Herb Leonard, who had been in the steakburger business since 1939 with Gus (and has recently celebrated his sixtieth year with the company), told of Gus' first ventures into cooking for the public. Service stations were competitive businesses. A nickel was hard to earn as the Great Depression deepened. Still, automobile traffic in central Illinois was on the increase as cars became necessities for many middle class people. Why not give them something to eat while they had their tires changed or gas pumped? Gus wondered. "Fill 'em up outside, then fill 'em up inside," was his thought.

Edith could cook the food, he could take care of the filling station needs. If there weren't enough motorists, he could always count on traffic from students at Illinois Normal State Teachers College, about 1,000 students at that time. And office workers in Normal had to eat somewhere for lunch.

Around 1932 Edith began to cook chicken for travelers stopping to purchase Shell gasoline. That first little restaurant, actually situated in an old house with a circular drive, served beer as well as drumsticks and wishbones fried hot, crisp and tender, done the Midwestern way. It was open from ten to midnight. You could get all the chicken you could eat plus french fries and coleslaw for forty-five cents. A glass of beer was nine cents more; beer was popular and began to account for important revenues at the cash register.

But a change in policy at the university, a change which soon became law, threatened to close down the Shell Inn. A friend of the University had died and provided in her will that her large estate would pass to the school—on the proviso that there be no beer sold near the school.

The restaurant would be put out of business if they didn't change the format. Hamburgers and other good restaurant items would need to be put on the menu, all charged for separately. And certainly the restaurant would need to expand—right away.

It was actually a natural step. The tire and/or gas pumping business was dreary and unimaginative work. Gus was finding himself irresistibly drawn to the challenges of the restaurant business. If an eatery were done first-quality, it could make money and be an intriguing business venture too.

Gus understood eating trends as few in the business did. Long-time associates told me that he may have developed his sound sense about what Americans like to eat by the frequent traveling he did in the Midwest. He ate at a lot of "greasy spoons," and he knew what people liked—and what they didn't.

Many of the roadside "joints" were run in a slipshod way, with indifferent standards of cleanliness and food quality. Breadcrumbs, oatmeal and even sawdust seemed to find their way into the hamburgers served in sometimes ramshackle old buildings calling themselves diners.

Hamburgers and hotdogs had become American staples since their introduction around the turn of the century. A quickly broiled or boiled frankfurter, plopped into a bun and slathered with mustard or ketchup, was a quick lunch for the fast-growing work force which now included women, or a hurry-up dinner for families on the go to the movies, bridge games in apartments of friends, or a "little ride uptown."

But the hamburger, especially, had caught the public fancy. Grinding beef and grilling it for a speedy sandwich was "the cat's meow" for people in the twenties and thirties who no longer had much time to prepare sit-down chicken dinners or suppers which required hours of cooking. Through this early Shell Inn experience, Gus learned something. Although there were plenty of restaurants in central Illinois which served chicken and beer, no one had yet invented the perfect hamburger.

What the country needed more than a good five-cent cigar, Belt reasoned, was a superlative hamburger. You could charge ten cents for it, though that was twice the average cost for a burger, nickel apiece or six for a quarter. "And they would buy a good ten-cent milkshake too. I knew it as well as I knew my own name," he later told his company president John Engle in describing those early days.

Gus had a sign-painter friend named Hynie Johnson who was interested in the growth of the little Shell Inn. In 1933 Gus said to Hynie, "I'm going to start a drive-in. I'm going to have the finest hamburger in the country and a real, honest-to-goodness milkshake. Customers can come up, park, and get waited on in the car. Or they can eat at a counter inside."

If that dream (one dictated by necessity) was to become reality, the bungalow-type house where the Shell Inn operated needed fixing up right away. He went to banker Walter Rust and managed to convince Rust that he could make his restaurant go if he had a little operating capital. What would be security for the loan? He showed the banker the furniture in his rented apartment, and the banker advanced a loan of

$300. It was not quite clear that the banker understood that that furniture was not really Gus'. The Belts had a furnished apartment.

Gus sensed that high quality, the serving of consistently good food, could draw customers in and keep them. As the stories were told by those who knew, he seemed to be the king of marketing geniuses, one of those inspired men who senses what the public likes and builds that instinct into a business.

One story that Engle told was about Gus' dynamic marketing instincts and persistent care for customers. "When one of the roads [Route 51—which ran from New Orleans to Madison, Wisconsin] was torn up out in front of the restaurant, and was sloppy and muddy, Gus would go out and buy half a dozen umbrellas and get several boys to help people get from their cars into his restaurant." Neither rain nor snow nor dark of night should stop the customers coming into the newly born Steak n Shake.

CHAPTER TWO

"LET'S HAVE ANOTHER CUP OF COFFEE AND LET'S HAVE ANOTHER PIECE OF PIE"
—Irving Berlin

And so a new chapter began in the history of the Steak n Shake. As money trickled in, working with whatever they could take out of the cash register and borrow from local lenders like Rust on a small basis, Gus and Edith re-did the Shell Inn as a drive-in. They went for black and white decor as symbolic of cleanliness and sanitation.

It was to become a theme for the Belts' life: much they owned was done in thematic colors of the stores they founded. A home in Daytona Beach the Belts owned was black and white on the outside, with white carpets fringed with black inside. Eventually they drove black and white Cadillacs. But those touches were years in the future, when Steak n Shake had become a profitable and popular venture. At first it was hand-to-mouth.

They took the gas pumps out, finally, and tried to channel with an exhaust fan the clouds of black smoke that poured out of the "one-lunger" furnace in the basement. The parking lot was improved to provide for the cars which would be pulling up and enjoying curb service.

The old Shell Inn became the first Steak n Shake, opened on that original site at 1219 S. Main in Normal, Illinois, in February of 1934. It featured an expanded counter and booths along the edges which could serve forty or fifty customers who wanted to eat inside. It was called the Whitehouse Steak n Shake because "white house" was a recognizable restaurant style in the 1930s, a part of art deco design that also was expressed in the White Castle hamburger places.

Soon people began to say, "I'm going down to get a Steak n Shake for lunch," so the story goes, and the Whitehouse surname was dropped. The Steak n Shake drive-in in Normal became a "destination" eating place, known by its name and dedicated to "the best."

And the customers were coming—clearly it was working even from the very first. They ate the steakburgers and went away satisfied. Word was spreading that the food was good, service quick and efficient at the new drive-in. Word of mouth has always been important in the food service industry, and word of mouth has stimulated new business for the Steak n Shake chain both then and now. They come, they get what they want, they go away singing the praises of the place and telling friends.

Gus' friend Hynie Johnson designed the logo which has become so famous. An original emblem for the restaurant was lackluster and plain, just a circle with the name. Sitting at a table with Gus, Hynie said, "I think you need a snazzier emblem. Let me try to design it."

The "Circle and Wings"® logo probably came from Stutz.

Hynie went back to Bloomington and arrived with a new, winged emblem. Though some of the pioneers in the chain believed it came from an Anheuser-Busch emblem on a bottle of beer they had been drinking at the table, I think I know where that winged emblem really came from. The Steak n Shake emblem is almost identical with the Stutz car logo. Above the center symbol was a saying "The car that made good," and below it, "in a day." A Stutz had won the second 500-Mile Race in Indianapolis in 1912 with Joe Dawson as its driver, and that had insured its reputation. Hynie had gone back to Bloomington, borrowed the Stutz emblem, redesigned it and Gus accepted it. It has become a part of the company culture.

The new drive-in Steak n Shake had a streamlined, art-deco look which was to become a general pattern for all the stores to come. Gus used a plywood mansard outer finish on the roof about four feet high and painted it white, using black letters for the sign. Using nothing but neon, he put up signs which said, "It's a meal," "Tru flavor shakes," "Grinding only government inspected beef for steakburgers," and "Genuine Chili." These slogans became the basis for all future marketing, and a performance standard for workers as well.

What was Edith's role in all of this? She scrubbed floors, washed dishes, and tested and tasted the chili recipe until it suited her. "Gus was the brains, I was the brawn," she used to say. They were a working team, but early observers concede there was a lot of pulling and hauling between them at times, especially as they began to acquire more stores and expand the original concepts into a thriving business plan.

Increased sales and customer enthusiasm showed Gus Belt that he had a winner. It was time for a second restaurant. Another Steak n Shake, a walk-in with eleven stools, soon

A. H. "Gus" Belt and Edith L. Belt, founders of Steak n Shake.

Gus Belt's first Steak n Shake at 1219 S. Main, Normal, Illinois, around 1940.

opened in Bloomington, Illinois in 1936, at 509 Monroe. A second Bloomington spot soon appeared on South Main. Early on, each established its own identity, but it was plain they were part of a chain operation with what was becoming a set of uniform standards.

Financing the growth was a continually pressing problem. Deals were made with local people for the Bloomington expansion: informal partnerships, cash advances to be paid off. Finally Mrs. Belt, probably reluctantly, advanced about $1,500 from her savings. She had been slow to warm to the idea of a second, then a third store.

The sum from his wife allowed Gus to buy restaurant equipment for that first Bloomington store, the walk-in one situated in a store front. A counter, a row of stools, some one-armers set close to the counter, a french fryer, a grill, a couple of freezers, and a counter made out of plywood covered with porcelain constituted the equipment.

In the new Bloomington restaurant, as in the Shell Inn, Gus wanted to continue to emphasize cleanliness. Board of Health standards for the food service industry varied from county to county if they existed at all. In 1934 roadside places could get branded as "Ptomaine Charlie's," just as the tourist cabins of the times would be derided as "Bedbug Bob's." So as he was expanding, he would continue a formula: white tile on the floor, black counter seats, a general black and white decor, and frequent mopping and cleaning up to insure a sparkling interior.

Then there was the matter of the burger. To draw customers to his places, now that he was expanding more than ever, he had already decided he needed to be able to distinguish it from the sawdust burgers people were wary of. Word was going to get around; indeed it already was.

Gus chose to buy only the best meat in Illinois, from Pfaelzer Brothers of Chicago. It came strictly refrigerated, in barrels with overnight delivery, three times a week. He began grinding filet and sirloin into the usual mix which would normally range, at least in other burger spots, from chuck and some round to lots of cast-off lean and fat beef. He called his own combination "steakburger."

And he decided to be straight-forward as well as market-savvy about it: he would grind the meat right before customers' eyes so they could see tender, juicy cuts of lean beef being freshly ground for the hamburger that would soon be grilled for their taste satisfaction. At the rush hour, he or one of his assistants would wheel in the cart with the steak cuts at all three establishments, when customers could observe that T-bones and sirloins were passing before their very eyes. As he bought more restaurants and operated them as Steak n Shakes, Gus Belt began to display the slogan that he believed said it all: "In Sight It Must Be Right."

Somewhere in these earliest days he had that insight which was to affect the financial success of the business. He began to charge for the quality he was producing for the customer. Ten cents, which sounds like such a low figure today, became standard for Steak n Shake burgers at that time. The strategy worked; customers were willing to pay a dime for a better-than-average hamburger whose taste and quality they could count on.

Belt also developed a unique grilling method. The lore has it that he traveled to a place called the Winsteads' Drive-in in Springfield and observed a successful grill there, then returned to institute the grilling policy for Steak n Shake: take a ball (now called puck) of the steak cuts, slap and flatten with a spatula on the grill to sear in the juices, cook about one minute to a side at 350^0, then turn and finish sear-grilling. The result was a flavorful, crispy but juicy burger with quite a lot of the flavor of sirloin steak. The grill had to be cleaned after each full load of burgers came off; this insured a fresh, non-greasy taste.

The sort of quick searing and quick delivery that Gus considered imperative to get the customers speedy steakburgers required an innovation in grill technology. Gus wanted the working man who was his basic customer to get his food fast—eat it at a not-too-rushed pace—and then leave. His motto was "Three turns per hour"—twenty minutes per customer, so you could keep the cash registers going.

That meant the food line had to work in a streamlined, effective manner to turn out burgers for plates inside, trays outside. Gus pushed the cooking line timing to five minutes—unheard of in those slow-food days. The grill line was tied together to get the food out fast—into the hands of the customers on twelve stools and in fifty parking places, and put them out the door. He also asked the waiters and waitresses to tally the bill and put it on the customer's table right away. That is a procedure still observed today, one which allows the customer to get up and pay—cash—as soon as he/she is ready. So the cause of speedy eating was well served.

There was one problem, though. The old cast-iron grills they were using from the Servrite Grill Company in Bloomington took far too long to recover heat. Officials of the Servrite Company shook their heads at Gus' demands.

"Make me a quick recovery grill," Gus told them, and it wasn't long before Servrite came up with a grill made of an aluminum alloy (plain aluminum was too soft) with a thermostat installed in each side and six burners, three to a side. Gus Belt had discovered the basics of cooking by thermostat. As for the cooking temperature, his experiments showed 350° was right. Any higher would be quicker, but burn and dry out the product. His grill may have had one of the first thermostat controlled cookers in the country.

Add unique, high-quality condiments and vertically-cut pickles, and you may be approaching the burger of your dreams. Gus Belt said, "I don't like to find all the relish and mustard and pickles in the middle of the sandwich. You don't get to them soon enough. You ought to be able to taste pickle in every bite." He devised pickles sliced long-wise in his method. And buns should be appealingly warm and toasted. Thus the "steakburger" was born—-and, more importantly, promoted in lots of ways. Cheeseburgers became a specialty, too, and he registered the words steakburger and cheeseburger at that time—but never enforced the trademarks.

The ratio of lean to fat for best taste was one of the standards Gus investigated early on. Without the benefit of modern nutritional measuring devices, he came up with an 80% lean, 20% fat content. "If there's too much lean meat in the steakburger," Gus used to tell his grill men, "the meat is dry. If there's too much fat, it tastes greasy. And that's the way all the lousy hamburgers in the country taste. Ours are going to be different." Eventually modern nutritionists agreed with that percentage.

But it wasn't just "Steak" (burgers). It was Steak AND Shake, and milkshakes were the second half of the formula. In the 1880s a man named William Horlick had invented the malted milk drink by perfecting a process which separated malt sugar from grain. It was offered on the market to be mixed with milk—a healthful concoction for children and adults alike. It had to be shaken hard to get the malt to dissolve—thus "shakes." By the 1920s enterprising soda jerks were adding ice cream to the milk and malt shakes, and Steak n Shake created vanilla, chocolate and strawberry.

Ice cream was expensive. Operating on a limited budget in his first few restaurants, Gus decided to make his own ice cream. But they needed a large freezer to store the ice cream. As always enterprising and ahead of the game, Gus became a salesman for ice cream freezers, and his wife became his first customer.

302 E. Green *Food for Thought*, December 1955.

Using the commission from that first sale to Edith, Gus made the downpayment for their machine. Then, soon after selling two or three of the things, he resigned as freezer salesman.

In the earliest days Gus became dissatisfied with the french fries served at his first three restaurants. He did his usual sleuthing, eating at other folks' places, and decided that thin-cut, shoe-string potatoes were better than the thick-cut variety. He also found out that if potatoes were cut in advance and immersed in ice water, they would lose some of their sugar content, and this would improve their taste. So that became a standard technique.

Herb Leonard has described the philosophy of "In Sight It Must Be Right":

We took great pride in putting on what we called a story of action. While other businesses turned to automation, we continued to make steakburgers by hand . . . right in front of people, in sight, and right!

Gus used to put the milkshake mixers in the windows of his restaurants so passing motorists would see them whirring and yield to the urge to stop and get a shake.

Each and every detail counted when you were building a tradition. Gus wanted an exact bun he had in his mind, with crust all around, fresh and soft. Arthur "Babe" Smith always believed he had devised the choice bun Steak n Shake has used for years. Babe was an early supplier, but there probably was another small-town baker who originated the custom bun. From earliest times Gus decreed that the buns should be one day old. Buns any older did not suit steakburgers—or customers—well. Babe Smith did join the company and stayed with it for three decades.

The fourth store in this budding chain was to be in Decatur, Illinois. Mrs. Belt's sister, Kathryn Hartmann, ran the store along with a friend of hers named Lucy, later the wife of Don Minick, a pioneer operator in the chain who ran the St. Louis stores and really developed the great reputation of St. Louis Steak n Shakes.

These were not large restaurants. Customers had to stand in line. Sometimes they tired of the lines and left, which bothered the grill men and store managers. "Never mind that," Gus said. "Nobody ever went broke turning people away."

So there were now four stores in Illinois. In the late thirties Gus purchased more already operating restaurants to expand his Steak n Shakes. Gus bought a restaurant at 609 E. Green in Champaign, and opened a Steak n Shake at this site. Two drive-ins appeared for sale, both called "The Goalpost." They had the same menu, philosophy, and cooking style as the Steak n Shakes.

Gus decided to open a second spot in Champaign. Located in the campus area, as the Goalpost, 302 E. Green, it was put into speedy operation by a man who was to become one of Gus' leading lieutenants, E.O. Blankenship. It was, according to him, "wildly successful," though it was closed in 1999.

Another Goalpost, 1150 W. Washington in East Peoria, was converted to a Steak n Shake operation in 1939. Herb Leonard was managing that operation, and that was when Herb began his long and successful career with the company. This East Peoria location on the river has always been one of

East Peoria store at 1150 W. Washington around 1940. Courtesy Herb Leonard Collection the most successful Steak n Shakes in the system.

The new restaurant had an interesting innovation. Peoria was what was called a "wide open town," with prostitution and gambling going on under the eyes of the local law authorities. In the foyer of that restaurant which turned out eventually to be one of the largest ones in the chain there were several slot machines which the company owned and operated for several years.

By 1939, when Herb Leonard was absorbed from the Goalpost operations and joined Gus Belt's operation as a supervisor, there were eight stores—that first one in Normal, two in Bloomington, two in Champaign, one in East Peoria, one in Decatur, and a recently opened Steak n Shake on Main Street in Danville. (A decade later a store was opened on North Vermilion in Danville and became a prototype for the expansion of the chain. It was to have nine stools, frontage of seventy-seven feet, and parking for forty cars—very important for Gus Belt. You must have enough space for cars, which really are your customers.)

The Normal store had opened with curb service. If "the curb" was done right, it could be a really strong marketing tool, something to distinguish the Steak n Shakes from all the other eateries which kept expanding all around him, Gus said.

Again observing other operations and reviewing his own experience, Gus decided to develop a training program which would realize his business goals. Curb service people were educated to "get going." They were trained to be swift, carry the trays above eye-level (for their own safety as well as for the look of it), and trot, so they could create a dramatic, showman-like effect. It was called a running curb.

The oldtimers always referred to the atmosphere of the

stores in the thirties as an important part of the selling effort—a bright and positive "carnival" feeling. "Four thousand of the little eleven-watt bulbs were turned on each evening. The round, bright marquee lights brought a little happiness into the dark Depression time," Herb always said. We still have vestiges of those marquee lights today in some of the stores.

Gus continued drive-in service and developed it in his own unique way in those first "stores" until it became a paramount and most important part of the business.

Drive-in service became the cornerstone of the chain's great success. In fact, 80% of sales were from curb service until the later decades of this century. Nothing has more appeal than having a pretty girl or a bright lad, neatly clad, come hurrying out to say in a courteous and friendly way, "Hello, how are you?", take your order, and rush back with everything on a tray, the burgers still piping hot, the Coke fizzing. It was one of the keystones of Steak n Shake's formula for success.

You could sit at the counter, you could eat in your car with the hustling curb girls and boys to wait on you, or you could Takhomasak, a term used to designate take-out service that Gus appropriated from a western restaurant. (Like Sam Walton, Gus Belt was someone who learned and borrowed from others. Good ideas are really not patentable, and most people are willing to share their formulas for success, if you ask tactfully.)

Gus visited a small chain of restaurants in Denver called the Rocky Mountain Hamburger Company. They had the slogan "Tak-Homa-Sak" printed on their wall, and Gus liked the idea. With permission from the president of the stores, he appropriated it. It too languished in later years, and that was something that caught my eye as needing to be picked up again as one of the great marketing tools of the early days.

CHAPTER THREE

"ACCENTUATE THE POSITIVE"—GUS BELT
—Johnny Mercer

By 1943 Steak n Shake had fifteen stores. A walk-in experiment in Chicago had been tried. It had not been very successful because the large city could not attain the customer identification factor Steak n Shake needed, and because of difficulties in the neighborhoods, such as hooliganism against the stores. Windows were smashed by rocks. The restaurants were closed, and Gus' stores concentrated on normal curb service.

But successful stores had been added in Galesburg and Springfield, too. And during this period Gus had opened and was running a successful store in downtown Hot Springs, Arkansas, at 601 Central Avenue, which continued there until the late fifties.

In 1943 John Engle came to the company and became the leading assistant and advisor to Gus Belt. John had been in the restaurant business himself, operating among other enterprises a lunch stand for railroaders and passengers in Galesburg, Illinois. He came on the team through the sort of casual associations based on friendships and pal-ing around that Gus was noted for.

Gus Belt had come by the railroad coffee shop in Galesburg during these later days of World War II, and begun to talk to

John about the recent problems involved in expanding the Steak n Shake concept. "You are running around here trying to please servicemen and regular customers all at one time, and I think you may be ready for a change. I can't supervise all of the Steak n Shakes, and I need somebody to go to these stores and be sure the floors are clean, the food quality high. Do you want to do it?"

John "bit" and came to work for Steak n Shake. "We operated out of the office, which was at the time two rooms in the back of another company, the Bloomington Wholesale Company," John told me. John Engle and Gus Belt were to work together for the next thirteen years.

The company structure in the early forties had Mrs. Belt as vice president and Kathryn Hartmann, her sister, as secretary-treasurer—at least in name. Blankenship had been pulled out of active company management and put in charge of the Champaign store. Babe Smith, who had become involved in the company itself after selling it buns, continued to function in management.

Gus Belt, of course, made all the decisions as to who would own or manage a Steak n Shake. He was reluctant to franchise, wanting to own all the stores himself to reduce complications and increase his own revenues. But he did adopt the practice now and then. The oldtimers said he would sometimes let a friend have a franchise, then find he had to take the store back when the friend's management skills failed. Peru, LaSalle, and Kankakee are examples of towns with franchise stores in the early days. None of them worked very well, and had to be closed.

In Florida one of Gus' friends wanted to have a franchise, and Gus granted his wish in 1951, only to find that the friend was unable to marshal the kind of work it took to succeed with a Steak n Shake. Gus had to take back operation of the Florida store. Later, under Ike Meyer in the sixties, the chain successfully expanded into places like Lakeland, Orlando, Gainesville and Clearwater, and Steak n Shake became an important stop for tourists and natives alike in a state in the farthest southern part of the country, far from Normal, Illinois.

Somewhere early in the development of the chain of stores, Gus began to sell the land and buildings on which the restaurants stood, and lease them back. Probably this was a result of his own expansion needs. Sale and lease-back was, and is, a very common method of financing units in a chain operation.

Gus asked a lot of his employees, and his enthusiasm was catching. Of course the success, financially and otherwise of the stores, drew and kept people. Steak n Shake had developed the reputation for putting out the best hamburger (steak-burger) in America. There were no two ways about that.

"Gus wanted high school grads who would work like hell and demonstrated complete loyalty," Herb Leonard recalls.

"And by 1941 or '42 we were really going to town," he added. The war put a crimp in the supply of beef, and of course, beef was at the heart of the Steak n Shake operation. Gus Belt had a large cattle farm, and beef was supplied by this farm.

The war was indeed a major threat to the restaurant business everywhere, because supplies like coffee, meat, and other basics were rationed or available in limited quantities. If you can't serve food, you go out of business.

Gus Belt had no idea of going out of business, and so he did what he had to do. Herb Leonard tells the story:

> *The war was a terrible threat to Steak n Shake. Sugar, coffee, beef—all the essentials were hard or impossible to get in a steady way. What were we supposed to do? Have no food for the customers? We had a choice—find a way to get the food or close. Gus thought of a lot of solutions. First, he knew "the man"—someone he could make a deal with. Gus became a wholesaler and received supplies of sugar, coffee and the rest of the things we needed. But beef was the biggest problem—all of it was going to the military. Gus bought his own cows. He got a 600-acre farm. Yes, we did bootleg cattle. Gus sweated over it, and took responsibility for it all himself.*
>
> *Nobody liked it but we did what we had to.*

He did what supplying he needed, but as soon as supplies eased, the cattle were raised for showing. Posters showing a particularly valuable prize steer, reputed to have been worth $10,000, were displayed on the walls of the Steak n Shakes. Customers pointed at them, believing that was the very steer that had supplied the meat for the steakburger on their plate.

CHAPTER FOUR

THE ST. LOUIS BLUE SKIES

—W.C. Handy, Irving Berlin

Nineteen-forty-eight saw the expansion of the chain into what was to become its prime market—St. Louis—an area that would host many of its most successful stores. In 1948 Gus Belt traveled to St Louis, to the German Hill area on the south side of town, scouting the territory for a site in the midst of this area of good, cautious eaters—value-conscious people who would respect the quality for which the chain had developed a reputation. Locating Steak n Shakes in neighborhoods of people who respect value and quality, and who will become repeat customers, has always been good for everybody.

Gus met the owner of the Parkmore chain. William McGinley, who had six deluxe curb-service restaurants in St. Louis. He dominated the curb service food business, was indeed the "king of the curbs," and it was going to be difficult to crack that market. Still, Gus and his associates were ready to try, and it was soon proven that Steak n Shake could dominate the scene.

The first store was 6622 Chippewa, and another location was soon opened at 4298 Chippewa. Both locations and the eight others which subsequently opened while Belt was alive, became known for cleanliness and continuous quality. The

German population and other St. Louis customers became loyal patrons. No doubt they appreciated the courteous note at the bottom of the menu, "Thanks for your liberal patronage."

McGinley, meanwhile, found his way to Indianapolis during the latter part of this period. Driving along 38th Street, he noticed a prime restaurant location across from the Fairgrounds. The Parkmore he set up there became one of the best known drive-in restaurants in the city through the late forties and fifties. It was not far from the Teepee, another Indianapolis landmark which was shaped like a Plains Indian teepee with large "poles" out its top, and stood at the corner of 38th and Fall Creek, at the other end of the Fairgrounds. Eventually, McGinley sold the Indianapolis Parkmore, and another chain, Burger Chef, bought it.

A new Steak n Shake store at the Vermilion site in Danville, Illinois, had opened a year before the St. Louis store was due to open. Since Gus had decided the new Danville store would be the prototype, it was used to plan the St. Louis store. The new store would be of hedite block, eleven stools instead of nine, but maintain the famous black and white colors. It was inexpensive to build, costing only $25,000 in 1947.

Using that Danville prototype as a model, Gus built three stores in St. Louis. The store at 4298 Chippewa soon became a "hot spot" in the chain and helped establish St. Louis as the most bustling of all Steak n Shake towns.

Gus needed even more capital when the St. Louis "explosion" was occurring, and he decided to sell more stock in the company. He sold it in central Illinois, and so Steak n Shake has been a public company ever since. It paid a dividend every year from the first public offering in 1948 until the late seventies.

Although there were minority stockholders after 1948, Gus continued to treat the company as if it were his, and since he was the founder and was so distinctly successful with it, none of the minority stockholders seemed to complain. They had no reason! During a few years, as the corporate records show, Gus paid out 50-60% of earnings in dividends to stock holders. Probably he could have put the capital to good use in the growth of the company.

The building of other stores during the late forties and early fifties in St. Louis brought the total to seven. Eventually, probably because Gus needed cash and wanted to be sure that after his death no stock would need to be sold by his family, he sold the St. Louis stores to an investor, Alvin Vittert.

By the mid-forties Gus Belt was a wealthy man. Truly he did have helpers: his wife, who remained active in advice and management, and men like John Engle, Babe Smith, Don Minick, Ed Roark, and Herb Leonard. These people helped carry Steak n Shake throughout the Midwest and beyond, always profitably, but Gus Belt was the driving engine in the growth and success.

He was also becoming known as a "character," one of those men who grab and hold you, figuratively, by the force of their characters and their strong, individualistic personalities. Stories abounded about him and were told to me in the seventies, fifteen years after his death.

He had a carousing side; nobody who worked with him would ever deny that. One morning in his Galesburg hotel room, after a late-night party, Gus heard two mechanics hammering and making outlandish noises in the body shop across the street.

According to Vince McMahan, Gus raised the windows and asked what the men were doing. The men yelled up that they were making $2 an hour to take out dents. "Fine," Gus is reputed to have said. "I'll pay you $4 an hour to quit."

When the body shop owner appeared with McMahan, he demanded to know who was paying his men not to work. The three men ended up going for a drink to talk things over. The friendship of McMahan and Belt lasted some twenty years.

Gus appreciated his people, and they stayed with him. One reason was that management in the actual stores was so sound, so founded on practicality and excellence of performance. Gus probably invented the hamburger-place equivalent of Henry Ford's assembly line. The grillman would take the steakburger puck, flatten and grill it; another employee would smartly add the lettuce and other condiments at the dressing table as ordered; and the waiter would whisk off the plate to take it to the table. Gus asked that each person in this work line say, "Thank you," when he or she received a part of the job from the person before.

Gus was a great "trash inspector," according to floor people from the forties and fifties. He carefully scrutinized waste-baskets and plates returned from table service, looking to see what customers weren't eating.

"The fries aren't crisp," he'd say. "People don't want soggy shoestrings. Turn up the fryer."

Gus had a way with suppliers, and could talk them into favorable arrangements, coming up with rare items during the rationing years of the war. He was convivial and always friendly, available for late afternoon chats and listening to their concerns over a couple of beers. Ronnoco Coffee Company, for instance, became the supplier of coffee when Mr. Belt entered St. Louis. Owed by the Guyol family, Ronnoco produced a superior blend of coffee beans. It is still used by some of the stores today.

Gus bought whatever he felt like at auctions or on sales/marketing/site acquisition trips, and sometimes the purchases were odd or quirky. He bought a safe which had a door blown off, and people shook their heads. "Sometimes you come back with stuff that doesn't make you look smart," his old-time associates would say.

"And that may be just the impression I want to leave," Gus would retort. "It's better not to be just too smart-looking. People don't think you're going to take advantage of them that way."

Gus claimed to be just "an old farm boy" for all of his years, and his habits tended to back that claim up. He was usually up by 5 AM ready to go. He micro-managed the various restaurants, traveling the roads with Engle. He was ever dapper in well-tailored clothing and looked, as some of his co-workers said, a little like silent film cowboy movie star William S. Hart. Store managers reported he never carried a notebook, relying instead on scribbled notes he'd make on napkins he'd carry in his pockets. "He was an immaculate dresser," Engle told me, "and every time he changed suits it would take him two or three minutes to change his napkins from one suit to another."

But he was astute in what he knew about the restaurant business—what had made his Steak n Shake a resounding success.

The menu was printed on large curb service billboards in the parking lot in big, easy-to-read letters. One of Gus' suppliers, John Marten, told me he was having lunch with

Gus at the Normal store when he suggested to Gus that he add the Midwestern favorite, the breaded pork tenderloin sandwich to the menu. Gus pointed to the menu board outside the window. "Young man, see that board? It has made me over a million dollars, and I'm not about to change it."

Opening of a St. Louis Steak n Shake at night meant spotlights and
huge crowds in 1959.

CHAPTER FIVE

"CANT GET INDIANA OFF MY MIND"

—Hoagy Carmichael

Steak n Shake was growing and prospering on steakburgers, steakburgers with cheese, chili and shakes, french fries and Cokes. Very few items were added to that billboard during Gus Belt's tenure. That remained for the sixties, after he was gone. Believe me, when we made a few menu changes, I did it cautiously. You don't tinker with an engine that's already running smoothly.

Gus was an ardent Democrat and active in the party. At some convention or another he met one of Indiana's (and the National Democratic Party's) leading lights, Frank McKinney, Sr. At that time McKinney must have been about forty-five and a terrific banker, a man who always said, "Come and see me and I'll help you out." And he meant it. Frank McKinney was involved in several business interests beyond the American Fletcher Bank. Along with Bing Crosby, he was owner of the Pittsburgh Pirates.

Frank met Gus Belt, and they became friends. Frank told him, "You've got to come to Indianapolis, Gus. We need Steak n Shake there." McKinney even picked out the first site in the Hoosier capital—the Dodd's Townhouse at the corner of Meridian and Westfield.

Balloons and pretty girls added to the opening of a Lakeland, Florida, Steak n Shake in the sixties.

A staff of over fifty helped open the Indianapolis store at 4105 E Washington in 1963.

Zoning in that primarily residential neighborhood was difficult, impossible to obtain, so the first Indianapolis Steak n Shake opened in 1954 at Eagledale Shopping Mall. Eagledale was a pioneer—the jewel of early "strip" malls in the city—with Sears and other good stores opening near the National Homes subdivisions that were nearby. They provided easy-to-afford housing for hundreds of World War II veterans and others who wanted inexpensive and comfortable new homes. Steak n Shake fit into that format very well. For many years it was a highly successful store at the corner of Tibbs and Lafayette Road, but has been closed since 1997.

That store was a counter store before a dining room was added. From 1934 to 1954 Steak n Shake, with a few individual exceptions, had only counter service inside its doors. Customers preferred curb service, provided by the chain in unequalled fashion. But if they wished to go inside, customers sat at stools at the counter, expecting, and getting the quickest service in the business.

St. Louis stores operating about this time were promising a five-minute meal, and sometimes delivered it in three minutes. Parking spaces were planned to correspond with the stools—so "we could get 'em in and out," as the oldtimers said.

But times were changing. The allure of curb service was dimming as, with baby boomers being born, family life became a focus in the fifties. People wanted to have the option of taking their families inside to sit at tables, and have a little leisure to eat their chili and burgers. The first store constructed with a dining room was the well known Steak 'n Shake in the 5300 block on Keystone Avenue in Indianapolis in 1956. The arrangement became more common after that.

SIXTEEN STORES IN ST. LOUIS 1964

And for all the stores . . .

—Each week 150 prime two-year-old beeves used

—3,143,000 pounds of beef a year. Entire carcasses, tenderloins and sirloins boned, ground, and packed under Federal supervision in the commissary

—1,500 pound batches of chili made each day in bulk and frozen. Beans come only from New York state

—400,000 gallons of ice cream made for Steak n Shake's exclusive use at 8128 Olive Street Road

—260,900 gallons of pasteurized milk used for the tru-flavor shakes

—15,000 tons choice Idahos sliced this year for Steak n Shake. One carload used weekly in St. Louis area

—14,841,800 buns made in special molds this year
St. Louis Post Dispatch ad 2/16/64

Curb service continued at most of the Steak n Shakes, but as the fifties progressed, zoning became more difficult to obtain for drive-ins wanting curb service. Neighbors didn't want the noise—the music from car radios and the rumble of beat-up Fords and Chevies of teenagers "cruising" the drive-in, circling endlessly around to talk to friends as in the movie *American Graffiti*. And, strangely enough, parents began to complain that their children were being "run around to death" serving speedy burgers to customers. The work of being a curb server was just too hard, they said.

It's still my belief that what really killed curb service, though, were the small black speakers which began to replace the car hops. The car boys and girls were the vital allure of the whole system, and electronic devices could never take the place of a lovely girl with a bright smile and courteous, personal service. Gus Belt had known that well, and anyone who knew Gus Belt would know he would not inconvenience customers with speed bumps. We didn't either. Steak n Shake had "curb captains" to control speeders, among other things.

In the late forties Gus got out of the cattle business at Rossville, Illinois, sold the farm, and moved to St. Louis, which was now, of course, the capital of Steak n Shake. St. Louis success and St. Louis procedure were becoming legendary. A man named Joe Greeson, actually a college professor whose erudite ways were a bit challenging to most of the others in management, was put in charge of training curb boys and girls and other help. His style of "a running curb" drew public notice in the chain.

Arthur Smith assumed financial management of the company, a position he held until 1969.

Gus began to decline physically in 1953 and experienced a

stroke. In 1954 he asked to see a doctor in St. Louis and after that visit Mrs. Belt asked John Engle to make arrangements to fly Gus to Bloomington in the company plane, which had been in use for a few years. (The plane was headquartered in Danville at the hangar of a man named McCallum, whose nickname was of course "What-cha.")

Gus died in the Bloomington hospital in 1954, and his wife Edith took over operation of the company. At the time of her husband's death, there were twenty-four units in Illinois and the St. Louis area and one unit each in Daytona Beach, Florida, and Hot Springs, Arkansas, with the Indianapolis store about to open.

In my opinion the best thing she did in operating the company for some fifteen years was—nothing. The stores expanded from twenty-seven to fifty-one, but the basic formula remained the same and the slogans, "In Sight It Must Be Right," and "Tru-flavor Shakes, Made the old-fashioned way," the paramount ones.

Gus Belt was one of the true geniuses of the American restaurant business. His formula was simple but true: provide and charge for the best drive-in or dine-at-the-counter food in the business, cook it expeditiously and in the sight of the customers, treat your people well and play to the public taste. And—don't experiment unnecessarily when you reach success.

John Engle continued to direct the company for Mrs. Belt, with a gradual expansion philosophy. When she died, there were fifty-one flourishing Steak n Shakes in states ranging from home territory Illinois to Missouri, Florida, and Indiana.

By the end of Edith Belt's tenure, however, one could say that there was a climate of uncertainty in the upper echelons of management. Perhaps the growing enterprise was becoming too much for Edith, even though Engle was acting as a successful president and advisor in guiding her. Times were changing. Fast food chains were beginning to flourish. Tacos, chicken, and pizza were vying with hamburgers for America's quick-eat dollars. Strong leadership was needed at Steak n Shake.

Employees recalled that Gus Belt had a plan which would eventually enable the employees to take over ownership of the company. Under Gus' plan, each year the Belts would sell some of their stock at market value until, after ten to twelve years, the employees would own the company. It hadn't exactly happened that way.

In January of 1969, the Belt family sold their controlling interest of 668,495 shares to Longchamps, a New York restaurant chain. The purchase price was $25 per share, a total of nearly $17 million.

The Belt family had held almost 53% controlling interest in Steak n Shake until January 28, 1969, and as a result of the Longchamps' agreement, controlling interest passed from the Belt family.

During Longchamps' ownership, the company's sales rose from $17,100,000 to $23,500,000 and earnings per share climbed from $.71 to $1.02. Although they made a lot, they also spent a lot, and sent the company in a direction which was not good for the long haul.

To compete with the fast-food chains, Longchamps attempted to set up a "Junior Steak n Shake" with fast food, an experiment whose time had definitely not come for our patrons. Acquisition of other restaurants which did not complement Steak n Shakes' interests also drained the company.

Larry Elman, president of Longchamps and a man I came to respect and like personally, made other moves, such as combining the interests and finances of the more elaborate Steak and Brews that Longchamps owned with the interests of Steak n Shake. His own energies were dissipated by the responsibility of other Longchamps restaurant interests. In 1971 dissident minority stockholders of Steak n Shake filed suit against some or all of Longchamps and Steak n Shake officers.

So after about two and a half years, and after acquiring thirteen new restaurants and experiencing some successes, Longchamps found itself under pressure from its banks. And, finally, my operation, the Franklin Corporation, had the opportunity to acquire controlling interest. We were to become the inheritors of the Belts' tradition.

Recently I ate lunch at a Steak n Shake in northern Indianapolis. The waitress had apparently had a too-busy day, and I'd had to sit longer than I'd like, unattended. As I was preparing to pay my check, I said amiably to an older man sitting nearby, "Service was a little slow, wasn't it today?"

"Never been any good since Gus Belt died," he muttered. I smiled. It has been forty-five years, but the shadow of the founder still hovers over the operation. It is a long shadow indeed.

Gus' signs and slogans made Steak n Shake successful. Good steakburgers and fun made kids and adults alike love it. Normal store, 1950s.

CHAPTER SIX

"IT DON'T MEAN A THING IF IT AIN'T GOT THAT SWING"—QUALITY, CLEANLINESS AND SERVICE
—Duke Ellington

"Steak n Shake?" I had asked. "The restaurant business—it scares me to death." Though confident I could take on the job (it was exactly the sort of challenge I was looking for), I was considering the difficulties, particularly in maintaining competent staffing. I really had known very little about the company when it was suggested I take a look at it for purchase. I had sold assets in the Franklin Finance Company, which had provided consumer loan services for people in five states, and was looking for a new enterprise. Still I said, "Get me some numbers." Seeing them, I was no longer scared. The stores were making money. Soon I would be in the midst of hot fudge, cheeseburgers, and chili in numbers I could never dream of.

After taking an initial look, I told the board of Franklin Corporation, "I hope we get the financing to buy control of Steak n Shake." And, to my surprise and pleasure and as a vote of confidence to the enterprise, bank support came forth strongly and the path was cleared for the deal to happen. Still, I had some reservations.

"I haven't seen any of these places," I told Larry Ellman, the president of Longchamps.

"You don't need to see each one," he said. "Cement blocks, stainless steel and glass with black trim. They're all alike."

In September, 1971, we met at 100 Park Avenue—in New York City—Bill Krieg of the Krieg, DuVault, Alexander and Capehart law firm, me, and the attorneys for Longchamps. The asking price for the stock was $9 million, and we had to do some careful planning to put together a deal of that size.

Steak n Shake was already a public company—48%. We wished to get controlling interest in the stock—52%.

My lieutenant in the purchase, and in the running of the company, was a very capable one indeed, a Yale graduate, Harvard graduate school man named Dick Seal. He had been Financial Vice President of Ponderosa and assistant to Howard Johnson, Jr., the CEO of Howard Johnson, so he was well prepared to help Steak n Shake grow. I became the man of the heart at Steak n Shake—he was the man of the mind. He was himself self-confident in all he did, and he could do most things well.

Dick, as First Vice President, an analyst of paperwork, was in our operation a fine detail person who supervised precisely the opening of stores and then looked over financials hour after hour to see if they were performing. I was the marketing man and the front man; he the financial analyst. That, of course, was a real necessity in a chain which would be growing quite rapidly. The sale was completed.

Returning from New York, I wanted to reflect on where the chain was at that point. I called in a few of the long-time managers and executives and it was from them that I learned the inside story of the founding—and what had really happened after Gus died.

Immediately after his death there was a period of confusion. The firm's accountant was elected president, claiming he had Gus' blessing, but he was quickly replaced by John Engle, a dedicated and well liked executive.

Edith Belt ran the stores with John exactly as she thought

8609 Watson Road, St. Louis, a remodelled Howard Johnson in 1971.

Gus would have done. "Don't tinker with the formula" was her motto. The oldtimers told me she was particularly hesitant about opening new stores. "I have all the money I need— why should we worry about the trouble of opening new stores?" she'd say. They'd convince her that long-time personnel needed new opportunities, such as management positions that new stores could offer. Finally she'd relent. But Edith understood the rationale and preserved the formula, and the stores prospered, even if the chain didn't grow.

It should be said that the Steak n Shake component of Longchamps had not suffered from the diversification woes the larger corporation had felt. It was strong enough to survive. Now it was ready to grow, with some challenges.

It was obvious from the beginning that in the years since Gus had died, the company had maintained itself satisfactorily, but needed upgrading in the business management end. Steak n Shake was run in a decentralized way, with some restaurants having a lot of autonomy. There were Division Heads of operation but no centralized personnel, employee training, or advertising. They had some signs on taxicabs, some billboards in Missouri, and Ike Meyer in Florida sponsored Bozo the Clown on TV; that was it.

The main headquarters, with by far the most stores, was St. Louis. It was here that Gus Belt had made his fortune, right there and in Illinois, his home territory. Longchamps had headquartered the chain in St. Louis. Large billboards advertised Steak n Shake as you entered the town, and people made pilgrimages, went out of their way, to go to the St. Louis Steak n Shakes. The twelve stores there were the stuff of legend. In one of the stores, in the early fifties, people recalled fondly that fifty boys and girls actually were running with orders. Al Maxwell was division manager.

There were groups of restaurants, quite a few, too, in Florida, under the division management of Ike Meyer, a real devotee of the Steak n Shake culture. And of course the division in Illinois and Indiana had Herb Leonard in charge.

It would be natural to assume that we felt a huge challenge from the fast-food industry, which had developed through the sixties into a major force in the American food industry.

Burger Chef had begun the revolution to fast-food hamburger dispensing in 1965; I had known the founding owners. McDonald's began franchising at about the same time, and now millions of customers were "grabbing burgers" at their counters.

There was at no point a real challenge to Steak n Shake from the fast-food purveyors. Steak n Shake's niche was established by Gus Belt in the public mind and was relatively unaffected by the coming of the "serve yourself" companies. Of course, every new competitor affects existing business to some degree, so we had to be aware of fast-food.

Later financial analysts were always asking me to define and occupy a niche. I told them we already had a niche—a forty-year-old one at that time and we were comfortably occupying it. In the seventies you could say we were not fast-food and not Steak and Ale. We were neither fish nor fowl but we were decidedly the people's choice for America's most popular food—the burger.

Our principle menu item had always been, and was still the steakburger. As we were evolving in the seventies, this item was being served deluxe on china plates by uniformed servers.

Still, under Longchamps there had been some moves toward faster service, and not all of them were good. Bright, chrome milkshake makers had been ordered. These were supposed to take a mix, add milk, and turn out insipid, watery milkshakes which would replace Gus' delicious, tru-flavor ones. Then too, the stores looked old; the former owners had scratched their heads about how to modernize, maybe get a new look, change the old formulas to compete in modern times. It hadn't happened in any significant way.

I absorbed the culture rapidly. I wanted to know more about Gus Belt, the Belt family, and the company's history, because in learning about them I would know what made the company successful and enduring. And the oldtimers gladly shared.

In spite of Larry Ellman's advice that I didn't need to do so, I decided to visit as many of the Steak n Shakes as I could, and what I found was personally appealing to me. It was all so right—so basically straight forward: serve the best foods, charge correctly for them, make the customers always happy. I saw all but one of the fifty-seven stores we had in the first month of involvement.

As a result of those visits, when I took over I emphatically said no to change—at least at the basic formula level. It was the clean-swept black and white look, the good, flattened steakburgers, the friendly service, the china plates on the tables, and the creamy, home-made milkshakes whirling around there before your eyes. Those were the things that made customers head in the front doors and come back again and again.

And, now that the counter-stool culture of the thirties and forties was fading and fast-food a reality sure to continue to grow and dominate the market, we had to insure that Steak n Shake could guarantee its own niche and maintain an identity as better than all the Big Macs and fast fries.

That shouldn't be impossible to do, I reasoned. After all, McDonald's was advertising, "We do it all for you," but if you thought about it, they didn't do much of it at all. You stood in line, you told them what you wanted, you took the food (not nearly as classy as ours) to the table, and you cleaned up for yourself. Steak n Shake was a restaurant.

And there was the nostalgia factor. Many of the people who were "regulars" at Steak n Shake (and we did depend on regulars and still do) connected the restaurant with good times in their past. It reminded middle-aged fathers of past days of happiness, dates, and a shared milkshake with their first girlfriend at a table. The TV critic Roger Ebert reminisced fondly in his column in the seventies about his group of teenaged friends cruising the streets in Urbana and stopping for steakburgers at Steak n Shake. Ebert was to remain a lifelong fan of Steak n Shake restaurants.

Many celebrities were fans. I discovered Hugh Hefner of *Playboy* fame visited Steak n Shake when he returned to his alma mater, the University of Illinois, for football games. Dick Clark became a fan when he visited the Daytona Beach store back in the fifties, and Dave Letterman, the Hoosier native and graduate of Ball State, had eaten his steakburgers in an Indianapolis Steak n Shake. I remember hearing Lee Trevino being interviewed after a golf tournament in Indianapolis. "Lee, what did you do last night?" "Well, I had dinner at Steak n Shake," he said.

When I mentioned my new association, people said, "I love Steak n Shake—don't change it." You heard it all the time. What a wonderful asset to a company—to be loved. It certainly wasn't a common thing. You didn't hear them say, "I love the Power and Light Company," or "I love First National Bank." That sort of reinforcement, which I heard out loud when I went into the stores I visited early on, was a morale booster for the employees, too. It was nice to be loved.

But all wasn't pie and ice cream in the company. (Although we did add pie—chocolate mousse pie and other types— during this period.) Of course not. It had been pretty competently run since Gus Belt had died, but it hadn't really expanded.

"The only real problem with Steak n Shake is that there aren't enough of them," I emphatically said. Expansion was a must. We needed to take Steak n Shake beyond the borders of its home territories. The problem was that the company wasn't organized to expand at any substantial rate. It just hadn't operated that way.

After looking closely, I had a list of fifty items I thought should be instituted to improve the corporate culture to prepare for growth. Basically, we wanted to modernize while preserving what was good. After all, it wasn't for nothing that men, women, kiddies and all their aunts and uncles got a dreamy expression on their faces when hamburgers were mentioned and said, "I love Steak n Shake." We had to preserve, to use and extend that love and turn it into more dollars.

First on my list of "must fixes" was small but symbolic. It was the matter of the milkshake machines.

Steak n Shake had three varieties—chocolate, strawberry and vanilla. It was a big feature of the menu board. Why in the world the former owners, Longchamps, had wanted to tamper with those delectable, creamy, icy cold concoctions so thick you had to take your spoon and dig to get the ice cream was beyond me. Had anyone up there at corporate headquarters before me actually tasted one of those fast-food milkshakes?

I told the employees involved that I wanted the milkshake machine order canceled, and if it couldn't be canceled, that they should find a way to sell the infernal things to someone else. It was done, and the little old machines continued their reign on the counters of Steak n Shakes everywhere.

Another more than symbolic change: Longchamps had raised the price of coffee to 15 cents and our store managers and customers were complaining loudly. We immediately re-instated the 10 cent a cup price.

I was conferencing with managers and owners who knew the corporate culture. Many of them had been with Steak n Shake from the days of the thirties. Right away I saw that Herb Leonard in Illinois, friend of Gus Belt and Division Manager of Illinois and Indiana, was a man of rare insight and wisdom about the company, as well as life in general.

I asked him to come to Indianapolis, which I intended to make headquarters for the company now, and become my Vice President of Operations. He and some other store managers briefed me and showed me the ropes. When they'd finished, and after my own survey before acquiring controlling interest, I could implement my list further.

And I could start with some definite changes in the food department, cautiously adopted. During the two decades before, some changes had been made in the menu. Egg sandwiches, ham and egg sandwiches, sundaes, "toasted cheese," and a "tomato and lettuce salad with thousand island dressing" had been added. People were asking about desserts for the menu beyond ice cream, and the oldtimers thought it might be a good idea.

Sara Lee, a fine company with home-made tasting desserts was contracted to provide desserts at Steak n Shake. We added cheesecake, cheesecake with strawberries, and chocolate brownie sundaes to our small list of sundae treats (including pineapple by now), again to be made with our French Vanilla ice cream and danish for the breakfast menu, to accompany the egg sandwiches. We chose the highest quality products, just as Gus Belt had done.

And there was a 20-30% jump in sales right away at many of the stores. The desserts were part of that. Employees were glad they could offer customers a good, new touch to complete their steakburger meals.

The steakburger itself was put under scrutiny. During the

years just before the seventies, a "super" steakburger had been offered, perhaps in response to the giantburgers those fast-food chains were advertising. "Let's make a bigger thing out of these larger burgers. Super steakburger will become double steakburger," I said, and, "Then let's try a triple steakburger. We'll sell more of these more expensive products."

There was some resistance to this idea, because it seemed to Herb, my Vice President of Operations, that a double or triple would confuse the grill people, But the bigger burgers immediately caught on and soon began to outsell the single steakburger. Today revenue from the doubles and triples is significant. The grill people have had to grow more savvy and sophisticated—and faster, I guess.

Gus' fries—shoestring, lots of them per serving—were being purchased from a special supplier in Idaho named Lamb Weston, and they needed to stay the same.

Coca Cola had been a prime quality choice and along with the other "basics"—steakburgers, fries, and shakes—brought us about eighty percent of our profit. I believed that Coke should not be tampered with.

The point was that I firmly believed the number one attribute of a successful chain store operation is consistency, maintained so that its present and future customers will recognize the store for *quality, cleanliness and service,* and all the factors that make for customer satisfaction. A chain can even be consistently poor in execution, but a certain number of people will frequent that store because they know what to expect. Steak n Shake ought to be at the top of the list of those who are consistently good—and I intended to see that it would be.

We added cottage cheese and pineapple salad at this point. It seemed to me that it would be another draw to Steak n Shake—a man could go to the restaurant and tell his wife he was eating "healthy food." Women loved the cottage cheese and fruit touch right away. For those who didn't want fries, boston baked beans were served in little pots, with an "orange freeze" (especially popular in the summertime) to top off the meal.

Customers still tell the managers that they have purposely chosen Steak n Shake because there are "more than french fries to go with your hamburger."

Chili had always been a special feature and money-making item in the stores. Gus and Edith had obtained a special recipe in their mysterious ways, probably from the chili-loving town of Springfield, Illinois. (An old man in his nineties later told me that he had been a restaurateur in Springfield in the thirties and had provided the Belts with the genuine super chili recipe.)

The chili, as it had evolved, was a savory blend of ground steak, beans, and seasonings which had to be slow-simmered in a huge stainless steel pot. Beans were cooked, and stored, separate from the meat. Gus had been insistent about that. And it had to be "folded" for a period of eighteen hours to achieve that famous flavor.

Chili had gradually evolved so that it was a variant of Mr. Belt's super-chili, anyway. For one thing, it had less fat. The original recipe had called for suet, and suet melted and pooled up on the top of the chili. Gus had always opposed any changes; when a friend had suggested, "It's too greasy," Gus had insisted that the customers didn't know how to eat the chili. "That suet gives it a special taste. These people need to put some crackers in the bowl. That will absorb the extra fat at the top. Anyway, I have made a lot of money on this recipe. People love it. I'm not changing." Somewhere in the period after Mr. Belt died, they had decided to modify the recipe anyway, taking out the suet. Now, in the seventies, the leaner chili went three-ways.

I wondered if it couldn't be added in quantity to Takhomasak. That brought up another matter. At some point early on, I thought we ought to emphasize take-out food. Takhomasak was almost forgotten, but Gus had thought it was important, and I did too. McDonalds and the other fast-foods were providing quick dinners to rushed working parents, and larger amounts could add up to larger tabs at the cash register.

But first we had to reinstate Takhomasak. That Indian-sounding word had flashed in neon on the outside of the stores in the earlier days, and as the neon signs wore out, they hadn't been replaced. So I had pink neon signs put out in front of the stores to advertise Takhomasak, and printed Takhomasak again on the takeout sacks.

Why not make large pots of take-home chili for Takhoma-sak? We could order large cardboard containers, put a pound or two pounds of chili in there, and have them ready to go.

Managers were reluctant. "We'll run out of chili," they said. Run out? That sounded like a good problem for a restaurant. Just make more and have it ready.

But you couldn't make it in huge batches. That was because of the turning, with huge spoons so that the flavors would meld and it wouldn't stick. It wouldn't be possible under that customized chili production system to turn out a lot of takeout. Later, they solved that problem with a new slow cooker kettle that didn't involve managers having to turn the product. But "batch" chili to take home didn't happen in the seventies.

The "orange freeze" had been a favorite for a long time. Gus had gotten the drink from a carnival. "Really a summertime favorite," an early menu said. It was made with ice cream and orange flavoring. We continued it, and added lemon freezes too.

Eventually we put in placemats to brighten up the tables—including food pictures which became a hallmark of our operation and a great marketing tool. Customers would point to the attractive shakes and burgers, shining in their photogenic glory on the placemats, and say, "Bring me one of those." These carried the Steak n Shake logo, which had been removed by Longchamps. It was important to have Gus' logo as a visual symbol at all times for those who would come in contact with Steak n Shake.

I thought, also, that we should concentrate on small touches to enhance the feeling of specialness—to show us in the niche above fast food.

Ketchup. That great, marvelous vegetable concoction for all seasons and all products. When I had visited that Steak n Shake on Keystone in Indianapolis for the first time, I had done a double-take on seeing little envelopes of fast-food ketchup on the tables.

Why not the best? Gus Belt had wanted the best. We put those familiar looking bottles of Heinz ketchup on all our tables.

Coca Cola had the same sort of product recognition. Many purveyors were attempting to get us to change to an off-brand cola, but it seemed right to stick with Coke. So I did.

When I visited Florida stores, I saw them putting whipped cream and maraschino cherries on the shakes and sundaes. I ordered this to become standard company policy throughout the chain, and to this day the appealing look of the shakes as they go by, dressed up like something out of a forties soda bar, makes customers' mouths water.

The reinstatement of the neon signs for Takhomasak brought up something else that needed attention. Gus' black and white format, art deco to the hilt, had worked very well.

It shouldn't be tampered with much. But it was a trifle dull for an age made aware of bright colors and "flash" from television and all-color movies. Why not add a touch of red to the black and white? So inside we "redded" up just in a few places for highlighting—a few red tiles in the floor pattern, and red table edging.

Actually, it was obvious that most of the facilities, the stores, needed remodeling. They were—well, shabby. Seating availability was very small. Even with the counter-stool-only format altered, with tables provided, the stores still could seat only forty or fifty people. Space needed to be doubled. Looking at it, we could see that if we removed the present tables and put in "two tops" we could add seating without tearing out walls and gain more efficient layouts. The expansion of seating, allowing more people to get into the stores at once and then out, was surely a part of the 20-30% sales increase we quickly noticed.

I completed my program of visiting the stores. In Gainesville, Florida, I met Tom Jones, a veteran of nineteen years of service to Steak n Shake. "You're unusual," I told him, and when he asked why I told him, "You're the first manager I've met who hasn't been with the company for at least twenty years."

These wonderful employees needed to be nurtured and protected. During the last year of his life Gus Belt had initiated a profit-sharing program for employees, and I expanded and developed that.

A rapidly growing organization needed a good in-house informational periodical. Gus Belt had had a "Steak n Shake News," but it had been dropped after his death.

It seemed to me the employees could enjoy sharing information and ideas, and learn about the company's ideas for growth through a newsletter that would appear regularly every few months. A house organ or company magazine can be a great motivational tool, with reports of sales and promotions from local stores, recognition of outstanding performance, and homey descriptions of Steak n Shake regular customers' visits.

Our new house organ, "Food for Thought," was well received by managers and all others in the organization.

Steak n Shake had never had a company handbook, and we began work on one which would include routine matters such as bonuses and working-hour policies.

I studied insurance and managed to cut the extensive costs the company was incurring. Steak n Shake, for instance, had for many years full glass and extended coverage on its stores. To my knowledge only one of those plate glass windows had ever been broken. If we'd been a greenhouse, we would have needed that coverage, which cost millions of dollars cumulatively.

An idea whose time perhaps had not yet come came to me. Before the time that company T-shirts became the rage, I thought we should have a gift catalogue. One reason was pragmatic—people wanted those fancy glasses in which we put the ice cream specialties. Why not let the public buy them? We set a price on shake glasses and the thick coffee mugs and added T-shirts, wind breakers, beach towels (which are now antiques and worth money). It was fun for a while.

On a more important level, we began steps to decentralize and departmentalize the corporate structure. New departments of Advertising, Personnel, Operations, and Purchasing were set up. Within the next year or two, I worked with Herb Leonard to set up a training center for Steak n Shake on West 71st in Indianapolis. The corporate culture, Gus' formula for success, ought to be able to be taught. In fact, it had to be taught so a whole new generation of managers of Steak n

Shakes in the expanded system could implement it. Thus the Belt vision was on its way to being made permanent.

CHAPTER SEVEN
STEADY AS SHE GROWS

The food production system had been reviewed and internal mangement procedures had been modernized. But what about financial records? We designed a whole new system of financial reporting which included profit and loss spreadsheets, operating statistics, and many of the other tools businesses in the seventies depended on, so we could really track the activities of the company.

Computerized cash registers were changing the retail industry everywhere, so of course they became standard at Steak n Shakes during this period.

An annual report was a must, and I spent all the money necessary to hire good design and graphics so as to put out a "class act" annual report with detailed information for stockholders. It seemed important to me to have the corporate report in the mail as soon as possible after the close of the fiscal year September 30. It went out in six weeks, an unusally quick reporting time to shareholders.

But customers have a vested interest in the company, too, of course, so we produced a "pocket report" to be placed in Steak n Shakes all over our network. With this "pocket report," customers could compare our record over the past six years, review income statements and balance sheets, and perhaps be encouraged to buy stock.

Finances at even the most elementary level demanded attention. The corporation at that time had large deposits in checking accounts. In the early seventies $2.5 million sat in non-interest-bearing checking accounts. Something had to be done about that.

I went to lunch with Indianapolis bank officials who had some of the cash sitting in the checking accounts. I left before dessert. I had to transfer that money from them to interest-bearing and other sorts of accounts which would make the company some money!

When I'd bought controlling interest in the chain, I'd said, "There's only one thing wrong with Steak n Shake—there aren't enough of them." Now that organizational changes were underway and substantial new hiring was taking place, we could specifically address that great and most important need.

I set the goal of adding twelve stores in 1972. John Wallace, one of Bud Tucker's partners in the F.C. Tucker Company, began negotiating for land for the new stores in Indianapolis, and Baker, McHenry and Welch engineers began drawing plans for a really contemporary look. The old blocky, white and black, wide drive-in look had marked the chain for what it was. It was a landmark in the cities and towns it appeared—easily recognizable, part of the ambience of the whole picture for the customers. It should be retained, but in an altered form.

What should the new look be? We were delayed in expansion for some weeks until we resolved the situation—by staying with the Mrs. Belt/Longchamps concrete and expandable store and adding a mansard roof look. It is the same look that prevails in the stores today across the country—bright and noticeable, untrendy but recognizable as a driver goes down the street. As is natural and appropriate, it is being replaced gradually today with an even more contemporary look.

It took time to get the sites, too. Site finders were hired. Particularly difficult was one for which we had to wait some years at Nora in Indianapolis. A strip mall occupied the land we wanted; the location was filled with businesses and service offices, but finally, and with $310,000 land cost, we had our dream and one of our most successful stores at 86th and Westfield Boulevard. Most land purchases were not that hard.

Growth implies advertising. Advertising had not been a priority for the company, but it seemed to me that the modern television-oriented customer expected to have it for name recognition, differentiation of product line and information about "specials" the restaurant could offer. Americans were used to viewing bright, show-biz spots with singing and dancing girls belting out tunes which were catchy and which were good come-ons. "You deserve a break today," pretty girls in McDonald uniforms sang as they danced.

The problem was, the ads didn't have much to do with the food service. We decided to go for clever in-store commercials which not only caught the viewer's attention, but also showed the quality of the appetizing food that would be served, and the help as well.

We established an advertising budget of two percent of sales for 1972—$500,000. That was a significant sum in those days.

What should it go for specifically, as we designed advertisements? First of all, it seemed to me that we could capitalize on the slogans Gus Belt had originated and which had in former days been closely associated with Steak n Shake. We should drop "We protect your health." That wasn't necessary in the day and age of Boards of Health.

But—were the rest trademarked? Registered? There seemed

to be some expense in the budget for a lawyer in Chicago for what seemed the enormous sum of $2,000-$3,000 a month for trademark protection—at least that's what I thought he was doing.

Attorney Jack Hanley and I went to Chicago to see what was going on with this lawyer and our trademarks. We met and delved into the history. Many key slogans had been registered to us. "Steak n Shake—It's a Meal" and "In Sight It Must Be Right" were indeed trademarked. But, oddly enough, Gus had also copyrighted the terms "steakburger" and even "cheeseburger." Of course, since we had never enforced this right or used them exclusively, those particular trademarks could not be claimed any longer. But the original, more important slogans were ours and should be used in an advertising campaign.

And so the advertising campaign to make the name of Steak

Steak n Shake News, July, August 1976

Mr. Steak n Shake—Jim Begg. An "out take" commercial showed all the mistakes he'd made while filming—dropping trays and spilling shakes.

n Shake a household word began. Why should everyone who wanted a break head towards a Big Mac? We were fun too. We wanted every home to echo to the cry of its family members, "Let's go to Steak n Shake. In Sight It Must Be Right. Takhomasak."

We hired Tatem, Laird, and Kudner of Chicago. Then, in typical keep-the-focus-on-the-burgers-and-people style, we chose an actor named Jim Begg to become our spokesman. He was shown in the store, demonstrating how the burgers and chili and shakes were prepared by clean-cut and courteous employees. It was the beginning of a kind of advertising that is at its best in the Steak n Shake ads of today—visually showing why the chain's burgers and other foods are top-notch, with top service and differentiating the stores from fast-food places.

But this was the heyday of creative theme advertising, and we decided to get creative too. I'd always been a circus buff and the stores, with all their bustling waiters and waitresses and activities and colorful customers seemed to remind me of a circus. Mr. Belt had emphasized a carnival-like mood in the stores in the early days. He put up bright marquee lights around the outside of the stores to suggest lively activity—fun and action. He had a touch of the "carny" in his own management style too—he told the employees to park their cars in front of the restaurants in slow times so customers would be attracted to come on in. Bring 'em in, show 'em a good time while they're here.

So we took on the circus theme, and the employees and customers seemed to like it. I even wrote a commercial with the theme line, "It's a circus."

Riding with one of the operating men to Peoria one day, I played the commercial for fun on a tape. "You ought to have calliope music back of that," he suggested.

Our float, featuring pretty Steak n Shake girls and our calliope, won the Mayor's Trophy in the mid-seventies 500 Festival Parade. The calliope travelled around to various Steak n Shakes for promotional events.

Food for Thought July, 1976

We began using calliope tapes and went so far as to have a tape-operated calliope built for Steak n Shake in Sikeston, Missouri. It became a standard at store openings and in the 500 Festival Parade.

One promotional scheme that was strictly my own and which worked well was a "giveaway." Unlikely as it sounds, we offered "All you can eat" free to customers coming in on two weekdays for two weeks to one of our lowest volume stores in an Indianapolis residential area. Fifty-one thousand direct mail pieces went out in the Indianapolis neighborhoods. Naturally we were beseiged with people taking us up on the free steakburgers and Cokes. Sales went up rapidly, from about $5,000 a week to $10,000 and continued to increase and stayed there.

One thing I did not do well at that time. Corporate head-quarters had been in Bloomington, Illinois, but it was a headquarters in name only. The treasurer of the chain, Edward C. Roark, had his offices in Bloomington, but very little else remained of what Belt had built there. The headquarters of the company with John Engel and Longchamps had been in St. Louis—the heart and soul of Steak n Shake—the best market for the chain.

I decided to establish the general offices of the company in Indianapolis. My own home was in Indianapolis, and many good stores and efficient personnel were there. It seemed as likely a place from which to run things as any. Perhaps it was, but I believe a certain piece of the corporate culture was uprooted, and in retrospect it doesn't seem to have been the best idea. Sixty percent of the business at that time was generated by St. Louis stores, which is a lot of money and power and energy in one place. But I'd always been a Hoosier, and I was reluctant to admit that St. Louis could be a better place to run a business than Indianapolis was.

We leased the twenty-sixth floor of the new Indiana National Bank building on the corner of Pennsylvania and Ohio. Those were exciting days, as we prepared to extend the visibility of the chain as far as we could. Even the phones were black and white in the office—white bases, black mouthpieces. Indiana Bell did not approve, but we did it.

All of this implied a significant restructuring of the corporate financial operations. I have said the company paid a dividend until a year before I purchased it. Longchamps had been unable because of debt to pay a dividend for three quarters, and there was litigation pending from stockholders over the matter. This litigation was withdrawn when I declared an immediate dividend on taking over the company. Confidence was restored, and stock sales began to pick up again.

It was not only stockholders who were increasing; corporate reports show that the number of employees jumped in a year from 2,703 to 3,097—a total of 394 people. Who were all these people? Definitely staffers for the office headquarters in Indianapolis, but also the store personnel. Expansion was underway, and we needed waiters and waitresses and managers and clean-up folks. When you "gotta grow" you "gotta grow."

The 1972 financial report shows a reference to the company being traded in the NASDAQ. By the time of my presidency, there were between 3,000 and 4,000 stockholders. NASDAQ allowed the new computer stock-reporting systems to show exactly what Steak n Shake stock (shown as STAK on NASDAQ) was trading for at a particular moment.

Steak n Shake stock was selling for between six and seven dollars in 1971 when I purchased control of the company for slightly more than nine dollars per share. We split the stock two-for-one and then a sort of odd speculation began. There seemed to be good faith in the market that Steak n Shake was going to be well run and expand—viewed as a necessity in the financial community. The stock, then, varied in price from $12 to $49 during the year following our takeover.

Interestingly, the number of Indiana stockholders began to increase in 1972, going from twenty-eight shareholders of record in Indiana to well over one-thousand by the end of the decade. Missouri stockholders declined; probably this had something to do with the lack of support for the new Hoosier management.

"But remember," one of the old-time Steak n Steak executives warned me during the early days, "this company is not about selling stock—it is about selling food!"

Selling food. It was going to be well for us all to remember that was our purpose in the coming drive to expand—the real necessity of the next decade.

The expansion direction we geared up now to implement found great support amidst both store employees and top management who had been with the company for some years. John Engle told me that he realized that Steak n Shake needed to become a "growth company." That is what we geared up to do, and what we accomplished.

How well did it honor the founder's dream? Engle said that if Mr. Belt were alive in the seventies, he would have been pleased, even honored, to have had his company go coast to coast. He always recalled that Gus Belt had had no greater pleasure than serving people in his restaurants. "What better tribute can a man have, than that his very life's work reaches out across the country to serve many!" John said.

Spreading the original concept—expansion across the country—was the call of the day. We were only following in the footsteps of the founder. He had died too soon to implement the expansion his success called for. If he had, that expansion would have been a big success too. As one of the old pioneers said, "If Gus Belt had lived, Steak n Shake would have been the McDonald's of the industry."

Three years later . . .

(Excerpts from 1975 corporate report Securities and Exchange Commission)

. . . Our first quarter reports were mailed to shareholders last Wednesday. If you haven't yet received one, they are available here today. As I said in that report, we are very pleased with our results for the first quarter because on a sales increase of 26 %, earnings were up 53 %. This is the most satisfying quarterly report we've been responsible for since I've been around . . .

Our first new Steak n Shake was opened in August, 1972; and we have now opened fifty-five new restaurants in these less than three and a half years. Numbers 113 and 114 both opened yesterday, in Peoria and Sarasota, Florida. This is now the second time in recent months we have opened two new restaurants the same day.

I had a concern several years ago, that the pace we were establishing might make it difficult to maintain the high standards of quality, cleanliness and service that were, and always have been the foundation of our company's success. I feel that we have not only maintained those standards, but that our good will overall has improved, been expanded and that standards of performance are the highest in anyone's memory . . .

The consolidated summary of operations in our report on page 10 shows we have a five-year compound growth rate of 19.3 % in total income and that our earnings have compounded at the rate of 17.3 % . . . in that report we present the results of six years of operations. If you just compare the income and earnings results of this management using the six columns for six years instead of the usual five, from 1971 through 1975—then 19.3 % total income average becomes 23.1 %, and the 17.3 % earnings average increase becomes 19.1 % . . .

I believe we are gradually getting and are going to get more and more favorable publicity on a broader scale than before, as we grow and continue to record favorable results. Perhaps some of you saw the write-up in the *Wall Street Journal* a few months ago. Just last week we received more space, and more favorable reporting, than anyone else, in the *Atlanta Journal* . . . As an aside, we are doing very well in Atlanta with all nine Steak n Shakes we have opened since last February and have had no merchandising promotions.

But after all, we are still at most a medium-sized company, but one with great potential. I believe the fact that after thirty-seven years the company, though financially very successful, had only $23 million in sales and earnings of 53 cents a share, and four years later had sales of over $53 million and earnings of $1.06 a share, certainly attests to growth potential.

And we only operate in twenty-five markets in the country, in addition to still being in business in only eight states, though we've doubled the number of states the past three years.

—from 1976 Report (Securities and Exchange Commission)

. . . In fiscal 1972, the company began a major expansion program. At year-end 1976, a total of 68 new restaurants had been opened. Twenty-three were opened in 1976 and a greater number is planned for 1977.

Fiscal 1976 revenues increased 26.4 % to $67,900,128. Net earnings rose 19 % to $1.26 a share. Over the past five years, net earnings have increased at an average annual compounded rate of 19.1 %. Net worth has increased steadily and now stands at $16,170,257 or $6.43 a share. Of the 2.5 million shares outstanding, 1.3 million are owned by Franklin Corporation.

Bob speaks at his first annual shareholders meeting in February, 1972.

CHAPTER EIGHT

THE CUSTOMER IS ALWAYS RIGHT

In 1971 comment cards were introduced—prominently displayed to let our customers give their opinions on our food and service or anything else they wished to talk about.

I had long believed that comment cards were desirable; I had used them in my former corporate responsibilities. In a restaurant setting they should be put out in a prominent place for people to pick up after they had sampled the food— decided what they liked about a place and what they didn't. The point was that the cards were out, obvious. You didn't even have to get any cards back. The restaurant had demonstrated that it cared about its customers and service. And of course, we pay the postage. Many companies don't.

I would take the cards home at night and read them to my children. Most of those cards around that time had some simple statement like, "Great food, great service," or "It sure beats McDonald's."

But sometime around 1978 a woman wrote,

Dear Mr. Cronin, You have now made living in Houston complete for an old St. Louisan—by bringing Steak n Shake this way. In fact you have been kind enough to put one less than a mile away from my home. The only problem is that construction does not appear to be moving quickly enough. Is there any way to get it built in only a week?"

The Comment Cards

I saved some of the comment cards from 1974:

"Nothing could ever improve your delicious steak sandwiches. I have tried all the others that are so highly advertised but none compare, as I am a fanatic at meat, my husband being in the meat process and packing business."
—Florida

"Build a Steak n Shake in Pasce County Route 19 near South Gate."—Florida

"Your food is good. Your service is good but needs more waitresses."—Florida

"Now, please!! We need a Steak n Shake in Sarasota!!! Please we really need one."—Florida

"Please don't cut your french fries so thin as it makes them too crisp."—Florida

"Make your french fry plate larger. The potatoes fall on the table."

"Make your french fry servings smaller. They fall off the dish."—A stockholder

"I think the waitresses would look a lot better if they were wearing a little make-up. Such as a little eye shadow and some mascara."—Illinois

"This is your roving Indianapolis reporter again reporting on another Indianapolis Steak n Shake. I recently visited the —— site and received prompt, courteous service. They even let me have some french fries when I was short some money."—Indiana

"Due to my opening a store in the area, I have eaten in your restaurant four or five times during the past week.

Your service is not only fast and efficient but the help is the most pleasant and courteous of any in a fast-food operation."—Illinois

"I bought a baked sugar-cured ham, hot. And it was all fat. I asked for a new one and they just cut the fat off and gave it back to me. . ."—Illinois

"Please add hot dogs to your menu for kids."
—Missouri

"I understand the increase in prices for your items because I agree they are certainly a quality steakburger and very appetizing but at the same time in paying these prices I would expect that the table I sit at has clean silverware which was not the case on October 30 at 12:15 p.m"
—Missouri

"Just had some chili-mac today and it was great! But will be moving to Indiana and I sure will miss going to Steak n Shake because I won't be living close enough to Indianapolis to go there to eat. So couldn't you build a Steak n Shake in Ft. Wayne? That sure would be nice!"
—Illinois

We will appreciate any suggestions or ideas to improve your enjoyment of Steak n Shake _____

CONGRADULATIONS - YOUR EXCELLENT
FOOD. MAKES YOU NOW WITHOUT
COMPETITION IN THE FAST FOODS
ATLANTA MKT.

Name KEN MEEKER   Date 3/29/15 / 2:30 PM
(Please Print)   Time of day
Address 4940 KARLS GATE DR.
                        Street
EAST MARIETTA, GA. 30060
     City   State   Zip

We will appreciate any suggestions or ideas to improve your enjoyment of Steak n Shake Don't change
Any thing. I Really Like
The service and The Food.

P.S. I can't Tell the
Time on youre clock
But dont change it.

Name Neil McComb   Date Apr 4-11-75 / Evening
(Please Print)   Time of day
Address 7604 Tiki Avenue
                     Street
Cincinnati   Ohio   45243
     City   State   Zip

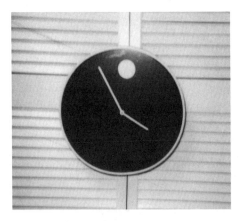

The "Museum Clock" became standard at Steak n Shakes in the seventies after it won a prize for the Howard Miller Company of Zeeland, Michigan, from the Museum of Modern Art in New York City in 1969.

The woman who wrote the comment card in Houston was typical of the many respondees when we brought one of the stores to their community. They acted as if a loved member of the family was moving to town. We had organized as a chain for expansion because growth of the corporation demanded it and because it was an exciting goal for all of us from the president to the serving people. But we were also urged on to expansion by enthusiastic fans familiar with the food, who wanted a Steak n Shake in their own neighborhood.

With a goal (overly optimistic as it turned out) of twelve new restaurants the first year of our management, we opened three in 1972, and then the chase was on. First was the matter of the town to be chosen for new stores, then the actual site itself. A memo I made in 1976 about locating new sites reveals the process in action:

> *I guess you're supposed to do a lot of research—how many would-be patrons are located in the neighborhood, are they the right kind to support the store—all that stuff. But I think you can pretty much tell by looking at the addresses on the menu of any one given store whether it will succeed, because the only important factor is high-density residential and decent commercial neighbors.*
>
> *Mr. Belt recognized that people grow attached to Steak n Shake.*
>
> *Once they eat there, they come back for more. And the closer they live to you, the easier it is for them to come in. A large part of our business is repeat business. It's true we need as a secondary tier of support substantial commercial—a shopping center with major retailers, office facility, factory, corporate headquarters buildings and even warehouses.*

And it's a plus if there's a highway nearby, so you get that traffic. But there's just a lot of good common sense that needs to be used here that goes beyond fancy projections on paper or done by computer.

In the seventies the White Castle chain was investigating locating their chain outlets in interstate locations, and of course McDonald's and the rest of the fast-food outlets were investing big-time in interstate outlets which have, of course, in today's world become very important.

I didn't necessarily want to see Steak n Shake go that route. My reasoning was that although we were well enough known and our reputation well enough respected to make a go of some interstate location or another, we hadn't tried all the high-density plus city locations that were beckoning to us. Maybe when we had exhausted all those possibilities we could expand along I-69, I-75, or I-95.

Not really I-95, because we weren't looking to go East. New England, New York, Philadelphia would have to do without Steak n Shake for a while. The growth pattern to those of us at the corporate headquarters during the early growth spurt years seemed to be South and West.

That meant we would eventually go into Houston, not Portland, Oregon. Portland was too far away from the center of our customer base. Lots of people had moved to Texas during the oil boom from St. Louis, Indianapolis, Atlanta— and they seemed to be potential customers. They already knew us, and there were some high-density residential areas, so we eventually took on Houston. But that is ahead of the story. First we put new stores into areas which were already proven as strong for Steak n Shake. We immediately began renovating and adding to sites in Illinois, Missouri and Indiana. This was done in '71, '72 and '73.

Then we moved in the mid-seventies into related markets—those we believed would have "immigrants" who would know us, or people passing through them with a knowledge of, and craving for, our burgers and shakes. Louisville, Kentucky, stores opened in '75 and '76 and Cincinnati, Ohio, about the same time.

Six successful stores were in place in Atlanta, Georgia, by 1975, and it was after that that we began to move to Houston and plan stores in Chicago.

So store expansion went forward in this way and became the driving force in the corporate headquarters, a great morale boost to those in individuals stores, for managers and for wait people and for the regulars, who stirred their coffee, ate their cheesecake, and talked enthusiastically to each other about "all those new stores in all those new towns."

It also became the daily challenge: how to manage site acquisition, construction which had to be done in a couple of months, opening and supplying the new places, and, especially, staffing. We had to move key managers who were succeeding in Illinois and place them in Houston. They in turn had to move their families, enter a new living area and new market for the restaurant they would manage, deal with new suppliers. Finding, training and keeping personnel at a high quality level became a challenge.

Some way it got done, and shiny new stores appeared. Their appearance caused other challenges during the growth years of the corporation.

One of those challenges was getting the training center on West 71st in Indianapolis functioning efficiently to provide the type of managers and assistant managers we needed for all these new stores.

The training center, which was being built at the cost of $400,000 (the cost of building a Steak n Shake restaurant at the time), was finished in about as expeditious a manner as was possible, though I was impatient to see it done.

Certainly the need had been great. In the years before 1971 the only way managers could be trained was on the job. When I asked long-time employees how long it should take to produce a capable manager for the chain, I was told two-and-a-half years. Examining the records, it seemed to me it took more like seven or eight years—at least that's how long these people had been working on the grill before they were promoted to manager.

That was far too long for a fast-growing chain. Obviously learning to grill steakburgers and buns properly was a primary necessity. But managing a larger dining-room store was more complicated than that. The government was constantly instituting and then changing the needs for employment, salary records, social security payments, health-department standards and licenses, and liability processes. The manager had to understand and execute these procedures. Personnel management was beginning to be viewed as a science, and the managers of a store had to personally orchestrate and keep in harmony a staff of some thirty or forty in an individual store. We weren't just putting down plates of good food on a counter anymore. The manager and his or her assistant needed to be something between a bookkeeper at an accounting firm and a father confessor-motivator like Bishop Fulton J. Sheen. These skills needed to be taught specifically.

Two-week sessions were organized on various subjects, and the managers and would-be managers attended, keeping the place busy from four to six months a year. I had been a primary mover in believing this training center stood for a new solidarity in the company. We could, of course, have rented rooms in the Holiday Inn to train our people, but putting the time and money into a permanent center said strong things about our commitment to the future. Still, it was a major expense, and the under-utilization of the facility was a worry to me and those involved with the project.

Curb people and waiting people were not to be slighted either. In St. Louis, Atlanta, and Florida, a part of the space in each store was devoted to a training room. Here tables were set up, trays put on a counter, and fake customer sessions were presented. "Sir, how is your chocolate sundae?" "Would you like to try the new salad, with three dressing choices?"

Organizing the new management in this training center was called for, and so I sought someone already at the top in the management training field in Indianapolis. Tom Altwies was Personnel Officer and Manager of Development at American Fletcher National Bank, and we approached him to plan and execute the program.

Tom was reluctant to come, so we offered him a vice presidency and gave him considerable leeway in decision-making, and he became our Head of Training. His job was to teach the corporate culture that had been so carefully developed by Gus Belt and his successors, and which we wanted to expand in a much broader fashion.

So people began to come to the center from Illinois, Missouri, Florida, and Indiana to receive their training. It was costly, but it was important to the future of the company.

The system of distribution to a growing set of stores in new parts of the country needed standardizing and expanding. By the mid-seventies we had warehouses functioning in Bloomington, Illinois, St. Louis, Orlando (with freezer space); Tampa; and Atlanta. Stores were serviced via trucks operating out of Indianapolis and Bloomington.

A commissary, a food preparation center and warehouse, had been functioning in Bloomington, home territory of the chain. We built a new building to expand that food facility which prepared chili, steakburgers and other staple dishes.

In 1972 the corporation commissary butchered 3,338,400 pounds of beef and froze 493,270 gallons of ice cream.

In this expansion phase there were some ideas which didn't work, some of which had been in place when we came in and some we ourselves put in—and which also flopped.

Longchamps had had a "Junior Steak n Shake" to directly compete with McDonald's and other fast-food operations. A quick-serve small steakburger, hotdogs, drinks—no chili, no sundaes, nothing more. The slogan, instead of "It's a meal," was "It's a deal." Dick Seal and I went down early on, in 1971, to St. Louis and visited the Junior Steak n Shake at 5:30 PM. Nobody was there. Sales at this bastardized store were $3,000 a week, $150,000 a year, maybe a third to a fourth of the average sales for a typical Steak n Shake then. It'd been open somewhere between a year and two years.

There was no curb service, which all the other St. Louis Steak n Shakes had. While we were visiting, a car pulled up in the parking lot and sat for several minutes—waiting for the car hops, evidently. Finally one of the counter men went outside and told the poor people that no one was going to come get their order.

As Dick and I left, we looked at each other and said, "Let's make it a real Steak n Shake." And that was what happened.

Soon that store was doing $5,000 a week and succeeding, even without curb service. I'll say it again—Steak n Shake never did need to compete with McDonald's and the other fast-food places. It hits a higher note, makes the customer rise, rather than go down to the speedburger level.

Our downtown Indianapolis "big city" store was not a flop, however. It was just different. It seemed to me that downtown office workers and visitors would flock to a location in the heart of Indianapolis. The location we found, east of the

Ultra New Commissary in Bloomington

——27,000 square feet housed modern, in-line processing

——CO_2 freezing system allowed steakburgers to be formed in advance in one central location: 30,000 steakburgers per hour

——beef carcasses moved into the facility and through entire process in one continuous flow

——truck docks were large, modern and efficient

Central part of commissary and accounting office.

Truck facilities

corner of Market and Pennsylvania was just right really, but it would not have enough floor space for our normal table service. Not expecting we could do the volume we needed to be profitable as a regular Steak n Shake, we opted for a walk-in, compact format, without silverware, or many amenities or much service. Just let the customer come in and order, stand in line with a tray, get his burger and go to a booth. I even got talked into the ketchup packages again. A quick service Steak n Shake in a high-traffic downtown area.

Although the store was a success as downtown office workers began to flock in, there was, clearly, confusion about what to expect. I wanted to call the downtown operation Takhomasak but didn't get it done. In spite of the fact that it only functioned well during rush hours five days a week, it began to do good business, serving something like 2,500 customers during the rush hours.

I dreamed of building a few of these downtown city stores during the next few years. They were to serve downtown needs, but the dream was not realized at that point. It was for a different generation to put Steak n Shakes in downtown areas.

Certainly there would be some experimentation and innovation as we went on our course of bringing Steak n Shake to all of mid-America. But it was to be a thoroughly exciting time for all involved.

And as always, the plan to spread the stores, dotting them on the map all the way from Iowa to southern Florida, from Ohio to Texas, would boil down to the creation of individual stores. State by state, we would use our model of Gus' formula for success to create good eating places for people. And they, the customers as individuals, would sit and sip the tru-flavor shakes, appreciate the best in steakburgers, in spots Gus probably didn't even dream of—or maybe he did! He had grown the chain—store by store after all.

CHAPTER NINE

SPREADING THE GOSPEL ACCORDING TO GUS

Steak n Shake under Gus Belt and throughout all of its years has been an intensely personal human endeavor. Stores have served the individual needs of their communities and customers. Cliché though it is, Steak n Shake is like a family. The following descriptions of Steak n Shakes state by state in the 70s growth period show just how human the restaurants were—and are.

"WE'RE LOYAL TO YOU, ILLINOIS"

The number of Illinois stores grew gradually during the growth period of the corporation in the seventies.

In 1973 in East Peoria, the site located on the Illinois River, was badly damaged by fire and re-built to seat 160.

The new store 3229 N. University in Peoria was the first store in Steak n Shake history to gross over one million dollars its first year. We opened 7715 N. University, north of 3229 N. University in 1972.

In Pekin, a good-sized town southeast of Peoria, we opened in 1973 a lively store which became very successful for the chain and still is.

In Galesburg, a poor looking converted store we had operated since 1938 needed upgrading, so we built 1066 N. Henderson. I once asked managers to tell us how to describe 1066 N. Henderson so customers could get to our store—one manager suggested "right next to McDonald's." We did not use the suggestion.

We built in '73 a store on Brady Street in Davenport, Iowa, just across the river from Illinois. We also opened a restaurant in Moline, Illinois on 23rd Street and these two openings gave us two of four cities in an area known as the Quad Cities. We had planned to open also in Rock Island and Bettendorf, but the first two stores did not realize sales and profit we had expected, so the plan was shelved.

In Danville a new north Vermilion store was opened in 1975 in a strong shopping center and the old dilapidated Main Street store was closed; the prototype store on North Vermilion was also closed.

In Decatur a new store on Pershing served customers' needs; in the Springfield area our good franchisee Hugh Stuller, whose father was a good friend of Gus Belt, now owned four stores, three in Springfield and one in Jacksonville.

Remodeling was done at 302 E. Green in Champaign and 708 E. University in Urbana, with greatly enlarged dining rooms.

For years Steak n Shake had talked of expanding across the river from St. Louis into Alton and Belleville, Illinois. This was accomplished in 1973 with stores opening in those spots, along with another in Fairview Heights, a little town on Interstate 64 with a couple of large shopping centers and not much else. Steak n Shake was a big addition to that community. It has been one of our highest grossing stores since opening.

Illinois Stores Existing or Opened during the Expansion Period were:

Normal—1219 S. Main (Original Store)

Alton—80 E. Beltline,

Belleville—4320 W. Main

Bloomington—604 E. Locust, 820 N. Main, 609 S. Hannah

Champaign—708 W. University, 302 E. Green

Danville—509 N. Vermilion, 705 E. Main, 3201 N. Vermilion

Decatur—1330 E. Pershing, 621 E. Eldorado, 802 N. Main

East Peoria—1150 E. Washington,

Fairview Heights—10860 Lincoln Tr.

Galesburg—1066 N. Henderson, 981 E. Main

Jacksonville

Moline—4241 23rd

Pekin—3205 Court

Peoria—4030 S. Adams, 2613 N. Adams , 521 W. Main, 3229 N. University, 7715 N. University

Springfield—585 St. Louis, 1580 Wabash, 210 S. Sixth

And in Davenport, Iowa,—4303 Brady

Burgers in boats: The West Washington Steak n Shake in East Peoria on the Illinois River allowed boaters to dock.

DOIN'S IN ILLINOIS SnS

3205 COURT, PEKIN

Women's lib was alive and well in Pekin. Not only did the Pekin store have women working grill and mopping floors, but they insisted on closing grill and taking out the garbage. Finally they challenged the men who unload the commissary truck to a duel of strength and endurance. They claimed that they could not only do a neater job of unloading the truck, but they actually thought they could do it faster!

December '75 Happy Birthday, Harry

Regular customers, especially ones like Harry Kirkpatrick who was sixty-two years old, were treated like uncles or aunts. Harry and his wife Alice were steady customers since the store opened (3205 Court Street Pekin). Harry came in every day for lunch. Then at supper time, Harry and Alice came in. Because of this double patronage, Harry received two cakes, two birthday cards, and two parties. Pekin Day Crew bought a card, signed it, and gave it to Harry along with a bikini cake. Kathy

Feaster baked two heart-shaped cakes and put them together. Night Shift also gave Harry a card and a cake made by Myrtle Pierce. Since Harry always ate his pie with whipped cream and cherries, the night shift gave him his own jar of cherries.

Harry and his Bikini cake at the Pekin store.
Food For Thought December, 1975

East Peoria store fire in November, 1973. *Food for Thought, December, 1973.*

East Peoria rebuilt in 1974. *Food for Thought, September, 1974.*

CHAPTER TEN

"BACK HOME AGAIN IN INDIANA"

—Ballard McDonald - James F. Hanley

Each store opening meant crowed counters and busy staff.

Indianapolis stores existing or built in the seventies were:
Downtown—108 E. Market

East Side
  7630 E. Washington, 8601 Pendleton Pike, 5401 E.
  38th, 1192 Arlington
West Side
  2660 Lafayette Road, 3810 W. Washington, 5635 W.
  38th
South Side
  7960 US 31 S., 2935 S. Madison
North Side
  5360 N. Keystone, 1501 E. 86th, 635 East Carmel
  Drive, 2960 W. 71st., 6360 E. 82nd
Lafayette
  Ind. 26 & 52 By-pass
Kokomo
  US 31 S.

The store on Carmel Drive became a personal favorite for my own family's dining out. I suppose I tested the waitresses' alertness when we ate lunch or dinner. Many times, even without knowing they were serving the president, they showed they could meet the customer's needs very well. But one waitress failed the exam. We had instituted the innovation of ice cream cones, and I said at the end of one meal, "My wife will have a one-dip vanilla cone and I will have a double-dip chocolate." The waitress looked puzzled and returned with Bette's cone. "I ordered a double-dipped cone," I said. "We don't *have* double-dippers," she slowly answered.

What was so hard about plopping a second dip on the first?

I told our manager, "Chuck, if you owned this restaurant, and a customer wanted a five dip cone, wouldn't you provide it somehow?

Mother's Day, May 9

2935 S. Madison, Indianapolis, had a lady take the sign on the roof "Steak n Shake Drive-In" seriously, floor personnel reported. Around 4 PM a crash sounded and the entire fountain section moved inward approximately one foot. "Smash and all, we remained open that day, but were closed the next day until a gas leak could be found. We thanked all the workmen who came out to fix us all up good as new." By May 12 the stainless was back in place, the windows replaced and the bricks all re-set. So much for "drive-in" service," they reported.

Food for Thought
July '76

CHAPTER ELEVEN

SHOW ME STATE STEAK N SHAKES

We often said our patron saint was—St. Louis.

Since Gus Belt had opened his first St. Louis Steak n Shake, St. Louis stores had become neighborhood institutions loved by the inhabitants. That was especially so in the case of young people. The stores were nicknamed by the kids for high schools whose students frequented them after hours and for lunch—Clayton Steak n Shake for instance. The staff, however, referred to the stores by their addresses—never even the communities in which they were located.

Howard Johnson's was faltering as a restaurant at 8609 Watson on Highway 66 in Webster Grove. Steak n Shake purchased this store and turned it into what was at that time the largest Steak n Shake in the world. A mansard roof was added, the interior remodeled after the prototype, and the Howard Johnson cupola sign was, of course, replaced with a large sign which ran the full width of the front. Opening day was a gala, with flowers, balloons, special customer awards, and many photographs. As a Steak n Shake, the store sales quickly doubled.

Older stores were remodeled and new stores added to the St. Louis area during the seventies. Other, old favorite stores

Four prominent Steak n Shake regulars at 1300 LeMay Ferry Road (l-r) Mrs. Hal Stuller, Linda Knight (Mr. and Mrs. Belt's grand-daughter), Mrs. Arthur S. Smith, and Mrs. Vera Stuller, franchisee.

were expanded. Typical of this process was the Brentwood store. Everybody in St. Louis identified with the Brentwood Steak n Shake. It had opened at 1104 Brentwood in Richmond Heights on June 19, 1950. Ace Martin managed the restaurant when it opened. Radio personalities, St. Louis county officials, sports personalities—all came by the Brentwood store to order steakburgers and shakes. It was so busy that curb service customers double-parked on the lot, letting each other in and out of spaces as they opened up.

In November 1977, after a long struggle, a new building was finally approved for the site and construction began, with Ace Martin supervising the job.

Key stores which opened in the expansion during the mid-seventies were 10459 Page Boulevard, 12607 Dorset, 13849 Manchester, 7310 S. Lindberg, 11035 Bellfontaine, 7606 Manchester, 13426 Olive Blvd., and 2221 First Capitol St. in St. Charles.

Other stores already operating or opened during the seventies expansion period were:

6622 Chippewa, 4298 Chippewa, 5828 S. Lindberg, 1525 S. Lindberg, 3549 N. Lindberg, #5 Route 140, 1253 Hampton, 12985 New Halls Ferry, 8609 Watson Rd., 9600 Highway 66, 9909 Riverview, 9860 Manchester, 7350 Gravois, 1104 Brentwood, 8660 St. Charles Rock, 7345 Florissant, #2 Crossroads Center, 1300 Lemay Ferry Rd., 3009 Woodson, 9009 Riverview, 8128 Olive Street, 9950 Natural Bridge, 6409 Natural Bridge

9331 Manchester

Springfield—1158 St. Louis, 1550 S. Glenstone

CHAPTER TWELVE

"YOU ARE MY SUNSHINE"
—Jimmie Davis-Charles Mitchell

The first store in Florida came about unexpectedly. Mr. and Mrs. Belt had a winter place in Florida, but because of gas rationing during World War II they couldn't get there. Mr. Belt built a store in Daytona Beach and got special gas rations to make regular inspections of the project and, of course, to stay at their Florida home.

John Engle, Babe Smith, and Chad Taylor had planned a trip to scout the territory in Atlanta in 1951, long before we finally opened a store there. When they missed connections and the locations turned out to be disappointing, the company officers suggested that they "go on down to Florida and look around and see Mrs. Belt."

This led to more Florida stores being opened in the Sunshine state. Under Bob Fiedler's, then Ike Meyer's leadership, eventually Steak n Shake flourished in Florida, on both East and West coasts.

In the seventies, we decided to stimulate sales in some unique ways. The Gainesville store had one of the lowest sales records in the chain. It was located in a college town; surely, we reasoned, college students ought to be in our Steak n Shakes, eating steakburgers and boosting our sales. To get their

The opening of the Tampa Steak n Shake in 1966.
Courtesy Herb Leonard Collection

STEAK N SHAKE IN FLORIDA
GAINESVILLE CELEBRATES GATOR GROWL NIGHT

The University of Florida's homecoming and Gator Growl night were always huge events for Steak n Shake. Gator Growl night in 1975 set store records for the busiest night, $2,131.29, and total sales, $3,281.56. They believed it to be the smoothest and best run day they had ever seen. The managers thanked all of the employees . . . Bill Blackwell, Alice Quesenberry, Debbie Sayers, Mike Maragos, Bill Conway, Paul Maxwell, and Gary Leach. Employees came from all areas of the state to help Gainesville out.

Food For Thought
December, 1975

attention and business, we purchased a Volkswagen to deliver food to the campus of the University of Florida. We offered a college scholarship to the athletic department, and soon athletes began frequenting the Gainesville Steak n Shake. And finally, we ordered a double-decker bus from London so students could ride to our store. Sales went up from about $5,000 a week to over $10,000.

Florida stores already operating or opened during the seventies were:

Bradenton—106 Cortez.

Clearwater—1698 Gulf to Bay, 2390 US 19 N.

Daytona—1531 S. Ridgewood, 945 Volusia
110 S. Ocean

Gainesville—1610 S. W. 13th,

Lakeland—819 E. Memorial

Largo—1978 US 19 S.

New Port Richey—1600 US 19 S

Orlando—1920 S. Orange Blossom Trail,
2355 W. Colonial, 2820 E. Colonial, 295 E. Altamonte, 4330 N. Semoran

Winter park— 8185 Orlando

Pinellas Park—4325 Park Blvd.

Tampa—5917 E. Hillsborough, 2315 S. Dale Mabry, 1450 E. Fowler

St. Petersburg—1020 34th, 2410 66th

Sarasota—S. US 41

Double-decker bus gets students in Gainesville and takes 'em to the
Steak n Shake.

GAINESVILLE HAD A TALE TO TELL
1610 S. W. 13th Gainesville

Gainesville had some excitement on Sunday, March 28th, 1976. A phone call from Macon, Georgia asked if a group could stop in for dinner on their way back from Disney World. The store people said "sure," and then discovered there would be 150 people on three big Trailways buses. They got together a few extra people and were ready for them when the buses pulled in about 8 o'clock that night. It was quite an experience in food service. A couple of the waitresses were running in and out of the buses checking for re-orders after they had served them. It was lucky that Gainesville was used to busy times. On April 25 the University of Florida had Joan Baez in concert. The stadium was packed, and so was the restaurant. "We got $1,485.60 on night and $2,350.00 for the day," they reported.

Food for Thought
July, 1976

POEM
(from #2 Crossroads Centre in Illinois)

The following poem was written by Lead Waitress Linda Henry. The busy employees reported it had been a great source of inspiration to them as they entered the Christmas shopping season.

Don't Quit

When things go wrong, as they sometimes will
When the road you're trudging seems all uphill
When the rushes are fast and the sales are high
And you want to smile, but you have to sigh,
When work is pressing you down a bit
Rest if you must, but don't you quit.

Life is queer with its twists and turns
As everyone of us sometimes learns
And many a waitress turns about
When she might have won had she stuck it out.

Don't give up though the pace is slow
You may succeed with another blow
Success is failure turned inside out
The silver tint of the clouds of doubt
And you never can tell how close you are
It may be near when it seems afar
So stick to the fight when you're hardest hit
It's when things seem worst that you
MUST NOT QUIT!

CHAPTER THIRTEEN
SEVEN COME FIFTY (STATES THAT IS)

Expansion did not stop during the seventies with the states where Steak n Shake already had a presence. The rapid expansion took the company into Kentucky, Ohio, Georgia, Texas and even to Tennessee and Iowa.

Stores at 9770 Montgomery, 8950 Colerain, 4646 Dixie Highway, 7991 Beechmont, 11470 Princeton Pike and 735 Lila in the Cincinnati area were opened during the seventies. The opening of our 100th Steak n Shake was in Cincinnati at 5341 Glenway, with officials flying in from both the construction side and from Indianapolis headquarters. Stores opened in other states were:

—Kentucky

Louisville area:

3902 Taylorsville Rd., 8215 Preston Highway, 9506 Taylorsville, 3232 Bardstown Road

Clarksville, Indiana—402 E. Highway 131

Site selection was not what it should have been at some locations, and at the end of the seventies advertising dollars were hard to come by, so the stores did not show the profit they should have. Late in the decade some of these stores were closed. In later years the company has had successful stores in the Louisville area.

We seriously studied offering twenty-four hour service at the Bardstown Road store near Louisville during the seventies. It seemed economically sound; a few staffers could extend the selling period through late-night hours and increase profitablity.

The Bardstown Road store was the first to eventually open twenty-four hours, and its increased profitability encouraged management to extend twenty-four hour service to all the stores.

Atlanta had been briefly considered as a site for Steak n Shake, as has been said, when Mrs. Belt was in charge of the chain. Now Steak n Shake pushed seriously into this promising territory in the heart of Georgia, with its growing cityscape, large workforce and burgeoning suburbs.

Nine stores opened in the Atlanta area in '74 and '75, six in the next few years.

They were located at:

2025 S. Cobb, 3880 La Vista, 2860 Candler, 3630 Roswell, 4537 Chamblee Dunwoody Road, 5690 Buford Highway, 3061 Buford Highway, 1418 Scott Blvd., 5400 Old National Highway, 4712 Memorial, 2860 Candler, 6623 Tara Boulevard, 3380 Northside Parkway, 2040 Peachtree, 2736 Cobb Parkway

After marked success in the first two years, a variety of causes caused them to lack enough profitability in a sudden "bottoming out." Still, the success of the Atlanta stores created an enthusiastic body of customers there and allowed the chain to open new Atlanta stores at a later and more prosperous time.

Tennessee did not have a store and we opened a store with the memorable address of 4266 Elvis Presley in Memphis.

Later, we opened three more stores in the Memphis area.

I had no question about our ability to succeed in any market where there were enough people to support our stores. We looked for a high concentration of stores in one good area.

Chicago was a logical next step. We had hundreds of thousands of fans in the area—people who had grown up loving Steak n Shake or from college experiences in central and southern Illinois. In 1976, stores opened at 1901 Algonquin in Arlington Heights and 844 Roosevelt in Lombard.

It also seemed to us that we should test a market where we didn't have the great number of folks who already loved the Steak n Shake experience. It needed to be an area with a dynamic growth pattern.

Customers who had become a part of the great Texas migration in the late sixties and early seventies urged us to move into the Lone Star state. We responded with five stores in Houston in '76—5745 Westheimer, 2227 N. Gessner, 3730 Kirby, 811 S. Gessner, and 5322 FM 1960. The lady in Houston who wrote the imploring comment card had her wish fulfilled.

From the annual report 1977

I think our 1976 annual report did a good job of highlighting the considerable progress we've made in the past five years. In my remarks here today I will try to give you some additional insights into our business.

Since fiscal 1971 costs have increased rapidly. In fact, this has been one of the few periods in recent years in which food costs have actually risen faster than labor costs. Largely as the result of our ability to pass these increases along to our customers in the form of higher menu prices, however, our restaurant operating profit margin was approximately the same per cent of sales last year as it was in fiscal 1971.

Between fiscal 1971 and fiscal 1976 we increased menu prices by 37 1/2 percent. During the same period the consumer price index rose by 43% and the food and food-away from home components of that index rose by 55% and 50% respectively. By any of these measures, therefore, a steakburger was a better buy in 1976 than in 1971. Possibly reflecting this fact, we have not encountered any significant or lasting resistance to our price increases.

During the last five years the average sales of Steak n Shake restaurants open for one year or longer increased 67% from $366,000 to $610,000. Price increases accounted for only half of this increase. The balance of the increase reflects an increase in the average size of our restaurants resulting from the opening of larger restaurants, the enlarging of older restaurants and higher customer traffic counts.

At the same time, however, we are continuing to explore new and better ways of holding costs down. We have instituted a manager's incentive program to encourage and reward our managers for better cost control and we have made increasingly effective use of our growing purchasing power—this year we are making a major investment in excess of $1,000,000 to install computerized cash registers in our restaurants.

Looking ahead, the opening of new restaurants is obviously the key to our ability to sustain and hopefully improve upon the record we have established. During the last five years, nearly half of the restaurants we have were in new markets. Nearly half of those restaurants were in the Atlanta market, which we entered only two years ago, and where our operations are already profitable. In Cincinnati and Louisville our operations were well on the way to becoming profitable before the recent bad weather. It is too soon for us to evaluate the Houston, Chicago and Memphis markets, but the results to date are encouraging. In general, our experience in new markets has reinforced our conviction that Steak n Shake restaurants can succeed anywhere there are enough people to support them. Our challenge is to make them profitable as quickly as possible in new markets and established markets alike.

Dick Seal

CHAPTER FOURTEEN

"SOMEONE'S ROCKING MY DREAMBOAT"

—Leon Rene, Emerson Scott, Otis Rene

And so, five years had passed since the effort to renew the founding vision, and greatly expand it, had begun. During those five years, as Dick Seal said in *Food For Thought,* in 1976, "During the past five years we have grown at a rate unprecedented in Steak n Shake's forty-two year history. We have tripled our sales. We have doubled the number of Steak n Shake restaurants in operation and opened a record number of new Steak n Shake restaurants in the last three years. We have reduced the time required to build a Steak n Shake from over 120 days to less than 60 in some cases. We have designed and built three new restaurant prototypes, our 115 seat Prototype I, our 155 seat Prototype II, and 80 seat Prototype III. We have remodeled sixteen older Steak n Shakes. We have entered five new markets in five new states: The Quad cities (Iowa) Louisville, Cincinnati, Atlanta and most recently Houston and plan to enter a sixth new market, Chicago before the end of the fiscal year . . . [We now have over] 7,000 employees."

Seal went on to list employee benefit improvements, the training center, improved marketing, and menu "additions," like onion rings and diet drinks. None of this, we all insisted, was bringing about real change. No, the steakburgers still had the steak cuts fixed before the hungry customers' eyes. And the shakes still had the cherry and whipped cream on the top.

Fifty-seven stores to 127 in less than sixty months. Seventeen cities to thirty-nine. From a population base served of seven million people to one of twenty million.

So, theoretically, thirteen million more people knew of us in just five years than had known of us before.

At the end of fiscal 1977, after six years of growth management, revenues had increased at an average annual compounded rate of 22.7% and earnings had increased at an average compounded rate of 13.4%. Dividends had been paid in every years since 1948 and the annual payout had been increased in each of the last six years.

At the end of 1977, the end of the first rapid growth period, Steak n Shake could count 141 outlets. There had been fifty-seven in 1971. Seven thousand employees were now on duty.

Expansion, with its many positive aspects, always brings risks. Those risks are implied in Dick Seal's report in 1977. It was not until the next year that we saw how the rapid growth of the company was affecting us in negative ways. Perhaps we did not fully estimate the extent of those risks. It had all happened so rapidly.

Chicago and Houston were disappointing in terms of sales. They did not realize the potential we had fervently hoped for. In Chicago I did not realize how important our advertising program had been when we had gone into other markets. Our Chicago advertising budget was not large enough to support the sort of promotion these new stores needed. The stores were doing fairly well, but not well enough to justify their continuing.

It was not long after we finished opening the Houston

stores that we saw the handwriting on the wall. We simply were not big enough, nor strong enough, to carry the cashflow in the red without its having a negative effect on the company's earnings. Marketing expenses were insufficient; negative cash-flow occurred and the company's earnings fell.

The winter of 1976-77 was a particularly severe one, cold, icy and snowy, and it was disastrous to our business in Illinois, Indiana and Missouri—the heartland of the chain. Unlike many businesses, the restaurant business cannot make up for lost sales.

It was difficult to believe, but the next winter was almost as bad; customers simply did not go out to eat much for long weeks. The State Police were urging them to stay off the roads. Our estimate was that each winter lost us over three million dollars in sales.

So sales plummeted when they needed to grow. With costs high and in the midst of continuous new building, we experienced substantial sales and earnings problems.

Often when costs are high and sales fall and the profit margin is off, people are inclined to say, "they grew too fast." I don't believe this is always a well thought-out analysis. No one has ever said Sam Walton and his Wal Mart "grew too fast." No, the process is more complicated than that. I believe it must be more closely related to management's inability to adequately control all the variables, the challenges that must be met and resolved during a time of radical growth—change. Some factors may be acts of God.

The entire organization of the company had had to change. Steak n Shake had an old, relatively slow growing organization. Many new stores were opened quite quickly; it was difficult to develop personnel skills and maintain high standards of quality, cleanliness and service. Those were the standards instituted by Gus Belt in 1934, and they were the standards we wanted. But with so much change, they were difficult to universally achieve.

We had taken the company several major steps farther in its inevitable destiny—to take its sound and satisfying formula for good eating far beyond the Midwest. Steak n Shake had become a household word in many markets. It remained for another generation of leaders to continue and improve on the successes that those in the past had won.

E. W. Kelley acquired control of the company in 1981 and has led it ever since. Steak n Shake now has over 340 restaurants in fifteen states. As John Engle once said, "Mr. Belt would indeed have been proud."

CHAPTER FIFTEEN

"THE BEST IS YET TO COME..."

—Cy Coleman - Carolyn Leigh

Fifteen states isn't all of America. We in the office in Indianapolis in the rapid growth years believed that Steak n Shake could be successful any place in the country where there are enough people with money. It still seems evident to me that that's true. Why?

(1) Experts have predicted that in the twenty-first century the hamburger will continue to be America's favorite sandwich. And Steak n Shake has the best with its steak-burger—over 50% steak cuts. It can and should be the Restaurant of the Twenty-first Century. And face it, we all must eat, so food service is always going to be a good business and necessity.

(2) Steak n Shake goes first class in the hamburger-based chains, with china, wait service, glassware and flatware. It has a trade-marked name for takeout service that's unlike any other—Takhomasak.

(3) Success since 1934 has been based on our Quality, Cleanliness, and Service—consistency in all things. These will be continued,

(4) There is a mystique about Steak n Shake and the way it operates. Customers today still love to sit at the counter and watch the grill man, affirming "In Sight It Must Be Right." I

think we know we're only as good as the next steakburger, which should keep us humble and improving.

(5) Steak n Shake has had an excellent financial record. It has had an operating profit in every year since our inception in 1934. Who else can say that?

(6) Gus Belt's dream was one of the great ones in American small-business history. And his dream will continue to be recognized more than ever as Steak n Shake becomes a household word as every single employee, manager, and officer remains devoted. The attitude of employees makes or breaks a company.

(7) Steak n Shake is an internet company, (www.steaknshake.com) and listed on the NYSE as Consolidated Products, Inc. with the symbol COP.

Thanks for your liberal patronage!